LIKE NO OTHER SOLDIER

ROB LEWIS

AD LIB

First published in 2021 by Ad Lib Publishers Ltd
15 Church Road
London, SW13 9HE
www.adlibpublishers.com

Text © 2021 Rob Lewis

Paperback ISBN 978-1-913543-55-6
eBook ISBN 978-1-913543-47-1

A CIP catalogue record for this book is available
from the British Library.

Every reasonable effort has been made to trace copyright-holders
of material reproduced in this book, but if any have been
inadvertently overlooked the publishers would be glad to
hear from them.

Printed in the UK

10 9 8 7 6 5 4 3 2 1

LIKE
NO
OTHER
OTHER
SOLDIER

This book is dedicated to my mother and father for having to put up with my various escapades. It could not have been easy.

AUTHOR'S NOTE

Like No Other Soldier is a true recollection of my life experiences since leaving the British army in May 1991.

Some names and identifying details have been changed to protect the privacy of individuals. Where real names appear, they are used in cases of historical fact and their inclusion is supported by independent, publicly available material.

ONE

I had filled in my voluntary discharge papers at army headquarters in Northern Ireland, Thiepval Barracks, Lisburn. It was time to move on to a new life and career in the civilian security and investigation world.

The chief clerk at headquarters had assured me that it would take about two months for the paperwork to be completed. I would have to attend a few interviews before I was fully cleared and debriefed, but I was happy just to have another few months of pay before I left for good.

I had already managed to get a year-long extension of the two-year tour I had done with the Force Research Unit (FRU). This was the elite, undercover military intelligence squad that ran agents during the Troubles – I have previously chronicled my career with this controversial outfit in *Fishers of Men*. Human resources decided I now had to either return to my regular unit, the Royal Armoured Corps, who were posted in Germany at the time, or transfer to the Intelligence Corps to be posted to a security section in England. I was not entirely enthused by either choice. For the past few years, I had been working undercover on secret operations gathering intelligence to fight terrorism and the prospect of wearing a uniform and having a short back and sides in the world of regular, tank-park soldiering was something that just did not appeal.

Don't get me wrong – I had enjoyed myself in the army and had made some great mates who would be lifelong friends, but it was just not for me. I could never quite understand why the military restricted the length of an operational tour with special duties. It took a significant period of time for anyone to work up good intelligence – Special Branch officers at the Royal Ulster Constabulary (RUC) took on their job for life. Obviously, that work came with huge personal risks, but it also led to large amounts of quality intelligence, experience and knowledge. As the old saying goes, 'Knowledge is power' – and they had that power!

There was nothing for it – I had to accept the standard way of doing things. I carried on with my normal operational tasks, carrying out covert surveillance and targeting, recruiting and handling informants while beginning the process of slowly but surely handing over my usual role to a new operator.

Informants sometimes become emotionally attached to their handlers; over time they come to rely on us for friendship, guidance and money. On average, I would make a point of meeting the informants I ran at least once a week to maintain a real relationship with them and now, gradually, I introduced my replacement to give my informants time to adjust to me standing down. Towards the end of that process I would only show my face at the occasional meeting, just to keep the sense of continuity. I was not involved in the debriefing process, which would be down to the new team.

I had various chats with my commanding officer about how I might carry on with this kind of work for other agencies – perhaps MI5 or even MI6. The Commanding Officer was a great bloke, he was a Lieutenant Colonel in rank and had previously been in the Gordon Highlanders before transferring into the Intelligence Corps. He had family links to the Fermanagh area and he played rugby for Enniskillen, a team that he was to introduce me into, and I played regularly for them, it obviously opened up a great social life as well. He told me that he would see what he could arrange. I returned to Lisburn headquarters and met with the senior controller for the security service in Northern Ireland. He seemed like quite a nice guy but was very dismissive about my joining his organisation. The majority of his surveillance operatives were little more than school kids, he said, and I could find myself in teams led by people who had far less experience and knowledge than I did. It would be quite hard for me to integrate into their structure. I would, more than likely, be London-based, have to make a commitment to weekend working at least three times a month and would have to live on starter civil service wages. He didn't put me off. I asked about having a role handling sources – there was bound to be an opening there, surely? The answer was that I would need to have been educated to degree level. It seemed to me that either he was being kind and didn't want to bluntly let me know that I was not appropriate for his organisation or he was being totally honest in suggesting the work wouldn't be a good fit, given my previous experience. I'd like to think it was the latter.

The next week we received intelligence from one of our sources that an AR-15 ArmaLite rifle was to be used to murder a member of the RUC. One of our sources would have control of the weapon and had been told to hold on to it until he was given a location for delivery – the address was to be given to him in person by a senior member of the Fermanagh and Tyrone Irish Republican Army (IRA) and we knew he would not have the time to let us know where he would be going with the rifle. His property was put under surveillance, with a covert van parked up in direct sight, while a motorbike rider and two cars covered the three possible routes he could take when leaving the area. I was parked in a quiet side street about half a mile away with the potential to cover two of his routes.

We stayed in position for two hours at which point, under normal operational practice, we would have to move on; it tends to get a bit dangerous to stay in one place too long. Passers-by can get very suspicious. Today, because of the need to keep tabs on the weapon, we stretched out a while longer. Everyone on the team was happy to continue as nobody felt that they had been compromised. We also had a Gazelle helicopter at our disposal for top cover; the helicopter was fitted with an optical sight operated by one of our team. If need be, he would be able to control the operation from around two thousand feet without compromising the ground surveillance. Helicopters were a regular daily sight all over the province and nobody really paid any attention to them.

'Standby, standby.'

The covert van operative let all call signs know that there was activity at the target address and everyone also knew not to say anything over the radio, to keep it clear until we heard the next instruction. The operator with 'eyes on' now had control of the task and we all waited patiently for his next radio transmission.

'Bravo one, complete with package at alpha one.'

The AR-15 was about to be delivered. We used the prefixes 'alpha', 'bravo' and 'charlie' over the radio to indicate address, person and vehicle. Radio transmissions were always in real-time: the operator in the van was describing the activity as it happened.

'Drop off complete and that is bravo two, in charlie one, heading towards blue two zero.' Our informant had possession of the rifle and was driving his own car towards the main road.

We used spot codes made up of colours and numbers to indicate locations, as opposed to speaking road and street names. It was more efficient for surveillance operations, keeping transmissions sharp and direct. Our source who dropped the weapon off was allowed to leave the area unhindered – it was imperative that his identity was not compromised and, as we knew who he was and as the drop-off had been filmed, he could always be picked up later. For the time being, we let the rifle travel to its next destination under surveillance.

'That is a left, left, left at blue two zero, charlie one now towards blue two one.' The van operative let us know that he had driven to the end of his road and had turned left towards one of the main roads out of town. One of the other car surveillance operators had that route covered and we soon picked up radio transmissions describing the journey, swiftly backed up by the motorcycle operative.

I had to cut across a housing estate and then speed up a bit to tag on to the rest of the surveillance team and wait my turn to take over from the operator who had control of the operation; it was quite a skill. I was driving at about seventy miles an hour through the estate in my haste to catch up when I spotted two police officers waving me down. One was holding a speed-detecting gun and the other had an M1 carbine rifle, a standard police-issue weapon.

I pulled over and one of the officers demanded my driving licence, asking if I knew what speed I was doing. My licence was in a clear wallet, along with my armed forces identity card. I explained that I was a covert operator on a surveillance mission, adding there were various weapons concealed in the vehicle and I was also carrying a personal weapon.

He was not concerned. 'Maybe you are – but you were doing seventy miles an hour,' he replied and started to write up a ticket.

I said that we were covering the transportation of a weapon that was going to be used in a murder attempt on one of his colleagues that evening and if he had any doubts about this then he should contact the head of Special Branch for the area, who would verify the operation. The officer looked at me. Then he returned to his pad, repeating that he would finish writing the ticket and let me go on my way. It was really quite unbelievable!

A local officer, who I knew, strolled over. He also told the traffic cop that I was an undercover FRU operator. This helped in no way at all. 'Aren't you supposed to be over there?' responded my tormentor, dismissing the other policeman back to where he had been covering a roadblock. There was going to be no quick way out of this. My ticket was issued and I had to drive back to base – by this point the surveillance team had got several miles away and I knew I was never going to be able to catch up. I radioed the operations centre and heard that the boss had taken the right decision. They deployed the helicopter and the weapon was still under our control.

I drove into our detachment compound, unloaded my weapons outside the building and wandered into the operations room. I was absolutely fuming. I discussed the ticket with my boss, whose advice was to let the process play itself out. I could plead guilty without attending court and pay a fine which would be covered by work. I would, however, have to take the licence points on the chin. I soon forgot all about the aggravation when he went on to reveal that headquarters had abruptly said I could leave the army right away. I was mystified. I knew I was leaving but I thought my exit would be another six or seven weeks away. Apparently, it was moving forward more quickly. Much more quickly: the Royal Armoured Corps human resources unit, based in Glasgow, had sanctioned my request to leave. I was officially out of the army on Friday. Bloody hell, this was Wednesday!

I had just forty-eight hours in which to hand over all of my covert kit, a variety of weapons in my possession and my operational car. At the same time, I had to pack up my house and get my last reports in. I also had to drive to headquarters in Lisburn for a commanding officer's exit interview and be back in time for my leaving piss-up at the detachment. The process confirmed that, no matter how important my role was and no matter how much I thought the system owed me a favour, I was still just a number as far as the army was concerned. Some clerk pressed the 'delete' key and, whoosh, I was gone.

It was all a bit manic, but I managed to get everything done. We rounded off the week with a pretty good team drinking session. The boss asked me not to return to the office and to ignore any of the other operators should I see them locally;

they had been briefed to side-swipe me should they see me. He said a few words about me in the bar and I had a painting and a bronze statuette presented to me by the detachment. Both featured fly-fishermen, as everyone in the detachment knew of my love for the sport. The painting had a brass plate inscribed 'To Rob: *pax vobiscum*', the Latin phrase for 'Peace be with you'. I had spent just less than sixteen years in the army, with less than seven years on active service in Northern Ireland, either patrolling the streets and countryside or as a covert operator. At the end of that last night, the detachment duty driver gave me a lift to town, we shook hands, said our farewells and parted ways.

I was going to be staying in the local area for a few more months, sorting out my CV and contacting a list of security companies given to me by the resettlement officer at headquarters. At my exit interview I was given three open, return-flight tickets by one of the clerks. They were all valid for six months and would come in handy for attending interviews on the mainland. I had also been given my regular army certificate of service – the 'little red book', as it is known in the army. My commanding officer wrote a letter of recommendation:

'Sergeant Lewis has had a very good career in the army and is now leaving to pursue a second career.

'As an NCO [Non-Commissioned Officer], he proved to be adaptable, resourceful and thoroughly reliable. As a SNCO [Senior Non-Commissioned Officer], he demonstrated a high standard of management skills. His decision-making was well balanced between common sense, fairness and sound judgement. He is well suited to middle management appointments. He is articulate and very presentable.

'Sergeant Lewis is a good team member and will be a valuable asset to any future employer.'

The army had assessed me as one grade below the top rating of 'exemplary' as I had been a bit of a rogue and naughty boy when I was based in Germany in my old regiment. I had a number of charges on my conduct sheet that meant 'very good' was really all I could hope for. It wouldn't be a problem. Most of the companies that I would reach out to had an ex-military hierarchy and employed similar servicemen and women. My experiences in special duties would more than compensate for not having an exemplary service record. In any case, I did not know many colleagues who left with the top grade.

From time to time I would see some of my old colleagues on the streets; we sometimes had brief conversations unless I saw that they were on an operation, when I would avoid them. I had chosen to stay in the province, and I had to deal with the potential risks of life in the area. I still had my army identity card, as the boss had forgotten to get me to hand it in and I thought it might come in useful in the future (I still have it, to this day). At home I kept a riot baton by the side of the bed. It was hardly the same as having a Browning 9mm pistol and a Heckler & Koch machine-gun, but it was still something for a worst-case scenario.

I had also kept back a flash-bang, a grenade that contained several smaller explosive devices that acted like mini-firecrackers, also discharging CS gas. This could be used to clear a room in close-quarter battle situations, disorientating anyone in the vicinity. You might remember how effective they were when they were used by the SAS during the Iranian embassy siege of 1980 at Prince's Gate in London. A flash-bang wasn't exactly what I would have liked to protect myself but, if I had to use it, it would give me valuable seconds.

Living and working in Northern Ireland was dangerous at the best of times, even when I'd had the full range of weaponry and communications at my disposal. I was now totally out on a limb with none of those safety measures; I had to live on my wits and take great care not to compromise myself. The consequences could be deadly. There were a number of people who knew me who had links to terrorists. My skills at anti-surveillance techniques had been well-honed and now they had to be perfect.

I was always very careful when I left my flat and I always made sure I was not being followed when I returned.

I sent out a hundred copies of my CV to a variety of companies and settled back to wait for interviews to come through. My leaving package from the Ministry of Defence included a cheque for five thousand pounds, although I had previously had to pay them two hundred pounds to buy myself out of the army when I asked for my discharge. Like a lot of things when it came to the army, it just didn't make sense. I hired a car from a local dealer who had been a friend of one of my former colleagues and I also secured my old fishing rights at a country estate owned by a friend.

Things were looking good – I had a few quid, a car and I could fish. I maintained a low profile around town and took care to avoid certain estates and roads – namely, those that I knew were home to terrorists and other personalities. The IRA would have been only too pleased to know what I did about covert operations in their area.

I had decided to have an evening fishing the River Brooke at Fivemiletown and had returned to a stretch that I had fished on a number of occasions. I had caught quite a few brown trout in the area before, usually around a pound or so in weight, but they were always good sport and great to eat. This particular evening, I was not catching anything, it was getting dark and so I decided to have one or two more casts and then head home. I spotted the telltale circles of water that indicated a fish rising and my fly dropped right in the centre of the ripples, bang, I was into what I assumed was a reasonable fish and played it for about fifteen minutes before easing my landing net into the water and drawing the fish in, it looked like a very impressive catch. I used my portable scales to weigh it and was amazed to see that it was just over seven and a half pounds, the biggest I had ever caught. It was a gleaming wild brown with red spots down its sides the size of my thumbnails, I decided to return it into the river. I had held it by its tail and let it just scurry from the bank and as I was about to climb up the riverbank and head to my car I slipped and went head-first straight into the river. I leapt out quicker than I had gone in but was soaked through to the skin, totally drenched. It is still the biggest wild brown trout I have ever caught.

I had been a Freemason for a number of years and attended lodge meetings in Enniskillen and the surrounding areas on quite a few occasions. One of the members of the lodge was a Special Branch inspector. He was aware that I was leaving the Force Research Unit and at dinner after a masonic meeting he asked if I would consider joining the RUC. I would have to go through the normal routine and basic training at their headquarters at Knock, Belfast, but as soon as I passed out he would request that I go straight into his unit.

I jokingly asked if I could have that proposal in writing. He laughed and said I should just trust him. Special Branch had been a constant thorn in my side for the past few years in my previous work, but the offer was quite interesting. I wondered if it was a ploy to get at my informants at the FRU – Special Branch were well capable of doing stuff like that – but I didn't dismiss the idea out of hand.

I was invited to the wedding of a cousin in Brixham, Devon, and decided to make a long weekend of it. I flew from Belfast to Birmingham and hired a car. On the Saturday morning, I took a stroll down to the harbour and, to my surprise, spotted the statue of William III, also known as the Prince of Orange, who landed there on 5 November 1688. He was to have a massive effect on the island of Ireland when he led the Protestant army to defeat James II at the infamous Battle of the Boyne on 1 July 1690, a date that is still celebrated by Protestants and still causes trouble in Northern Ireland over three hundred years later, in the form of the loyalist marching season. The marches provide major flash points for both the Protestant and the Catholic communities and have ended up with riots taking place in larger cities like Belfast and Londonderry.

I was sitting on the harbour wall, smoking a cigarette and drinking a cup of coffee, when I spotted a newspaper stand. A front page showed images of three people I knew and the headline made my guts wrench. A Chinook helicopter had been flying the top brass of Northern Ireland's military intelligence, Special Branch and the security services to Scotland when it crashed, killing all twenty-nine people on board – four crew and the passengers. I had been aware of this regular 'Junta' meeting, as it was nicknamed, which took place outside the province every month. The photographs showed Major George Williams and Captain Roy Pugh – my operations officer and intelligence officer at the FRU. I had played rugby with Roy Pugh and knew him really well; he had been a good man. The image was released by headquarters, taken at an FRU function. I was in the main photograph that it came from.

I bought a copy of the paper and headed back to my hotel room. My partner took one look at me and asked if I had seen a ghost – I was drained of colour. I read the coverage of the June 1994 crash in full and was even more shocked to realise the dead included that Special Branch officer who had approached me about joining his unit. I got through the weekend as best I could and flew back to Northern Ireland to continue my search for work.

TWO

I had no replies from my one hundred letters and CV applications for months. At last, a single envelope arrived. Finally – a response. But I was swiftly disappointed.

A Bristol company called International Security Services (ISS) thanked me for my details and asked if they could keep my details on their database, promising to be in touch if anything suitable was to arise. It seemed that all the work I had put in to applications had been for nothing.

I decided to spend the evening fishing, threw my fly rod and waders onto the back seat of the car and headed out to the River Brooke at Colebrooke, a lovely estate near Fivemiletown. I had once lived there and knew it was a relatively safe place; there were army and police patrols around and lots of members of the Ulster Defence Regiment and the RUC lived in the area. En route, I spotted a face from my past parked up in a car. This man had been a potential target for recruitment and I had worked on him relentlessly. Intrigue got the better of my common sense and I doubled back to park where I could observe what he was up to.

About ten minutes passed before two men drove into the car park, one getting out of their vehicle to join the first man. I knew the two blokes to be Special Branch officers. They were obviously up to their usual tricks and were sneaking my old target away from the FRU detachment. Bastards! I thought about calling my old firm but, sighing and with a slight laugh at myself, I chose not to. I was not working for them anymore; it was none of my business now. I continued to the river and, more satisfyingly, returned home with two rather nice sized, wild brown trout for supper.

The bloke in the car was later tried and found guilty of involvement in the infamous Omagh bombing of 1998 but would be released on appeal. The Gardai, the Irish police in the republic, were found guilty of forging notes on the case and he was acquitted. The police ombudsman would investigate the role of Special Branch during this period and find them sadly lacking in picking up prior warnings of this attack.

I had a good friend who was caught up in the bombing itself. He owned a clothes shop in the high street and was standing outside it, unaware he was next to the car containing the explosives, when the bomb was detonated. My friend was blown through his own shop-front window and hit a clothes rack. His eardrums were damaged and he was profoundly deaf for months afterwards, but he was relatively unscathed: the owner of a neighbouring shop he had been chatting with was blown into a wall and died instantly.

ISS got back in touch to discuss freelance work. I jumped at the chance and flew from Aldergrove airport on the outskirts of Belfast to Birmingham and then went by train to Bristol. I arrived the night before – my funds were starting to run low but I did not want to be late for this interview, which I felt could just be the opening I was looking for. It was also the only opening that had been offered.

I arrived smartly dressed and introduced myself to the receptionist. She looked at me blankly and told me that Mr Robson, the managing director, was away for the rest of the week. She said there had obviously been a misunderstanding or mix up on the dates. I had to hide my fury – I had used up one of my precious return tickets and had put a strain on my bank account to chase a red herring. I began the long journey home with the receptionist having promised me faithfully that she would get the MD to contact me immediately on his return. I rang him myself the following week as I was convinced I would never hear from them. He was extremely apologetic and told me that they had a firm job offer and that I could start immediately. I was suspicious to be made an offer without an interview but needed the work. I had no choice but to take the chance. I didn't even know what the job involved or even how much I would get; it was all a bit crazy.

I booked into a bit of a dodgy bed and breakfast in the notorious St Paul's district of Bristol. I knew the area reasonably well as I had carried out some joint training undercover exercises with Special Branch there when I was at 14 INT, an army covert surveillance unit. It was one of the toughest areas to work and provided excellent training as there was a lot of drug-related crime and many of the people on the streets were all very surveillance-aware.

On my first day I met two ex-Avon and Somerset police officers. They had started the company and chatted about my background and situation. I was to work undercover in a retail outlet in Bristol city centre, detecting shoplifters and thieves. They also provided uniformed security. It all seemed fine – the wages weren't great but at least I was going to be doing something. I headed off to introduce myself to the manager and the uniformed security guard, Brian, before wandering around the shop, using the CCTV and learning about the main shoplifters; to my surprise, there were a lot of them. Gangs of teenage girls would send two or three of their members in to harass and threaten the staff on the till to provide cover for others who would help themselves. They were quite open: they let the staff know they were going to steal stock and warned that, if they were stopped, they would 'see them' outside when the shop closed. It was effectively intimidating, but I had very little opportunity to do anything about it.

Towards the end of the week Pat Robson turned up to say the retail company – one of the biggest in the UK – could not even afford to employ a store detective and my duties would be covered by the store manager. I was out of a job almost as soon as I got it, pretty much broke and had nowhere to live. Robson told me that some uniformed staff, including Brian, lived communally in a large, empty building near Temple Meads railway station. He was sure that I could move in there until another job arose.

I picked up my belongings and Brian took me on a stroll down through the city and over the river to Temple Meads to my new home. There would be no rent to pay here – mind you, there was no hot running water or front door key. I was to learn the art of squatting! A situation in which I could never have previously seen myself.

Brian eased the heavy wooden door of the imposing Victorian building open a few inches, inserting his hand through a gap to push away a plank of wood that held the door shut. I followed him up a flight of large open stairs covered in worn carpet and Brian pointed to a door, indicating my room. The room stank of damp, had a threadbare carpet, no curtains and dodgy floorboards that felt sponge-like and soggy underfoot. I had the feeling I would end up in the room below if I didn't tread carefully. This was about as bad as it could get! But I wasn't the only one in this position. Brian said that most of the people in the squat were ex-forces; he had been in the Royal Navy for nine years and had been living here for over a year.

Brian advised that most of the guys took their valuables to the left luggage or lost property offices at the station where the woman in charge, herself ex-forces, looked after them for free. There was a sports centre on Temple Way where one of the staff was ex-Army Physical Training Corps and allowed us to use the showers. It was good to see that the strong bonds in the forces and veteran community still existed. This was one small silver lining in an otherwise very gloomy outlook.

The next few weeks were spent wandering the streets of Bristol. I was amazed at the amount of cash that had been abandoned, both coins and notes, lying in gutters, especially outside pubs and nightclubs. Checking cash point machines on my travels, I was surprised at the number of times I came across ten- and twenty-pound notes ignored in the dispenser. This was just about enough, allowing me to see my way through the day with a bag of chips each evening, rolling my own cigarettes instead of buying them in packets.

Eventually, the two blokes who ran the company visited the squat. They offered me undercover work in a warehouse, infiltrating the workforce to report on the theft of cigarettes and alcohol. This was what was termed 'shrinkage' in the industry and most firms allowed for a certain amount. This warehouse was suffering a small epidemic and they needed to know who the culprits were.

I attended a staged interview for a job as a regular warehouse operative. The managing director and the security manager for the group were the only people who were aware of my true role. As far as anyone else was concerned, I had answered an advertisement in the jobcentre. From my own knowledge of this type of work I thought that I would be paid the salary for doing the actual work and a sizeable consultancy fee for my covert assignment. As it was, they were offering only a hundred pounds a week over the regular pay – but I knew it was that or back to looking around the ground for small change. Robson assured me this was a new contract and they would get more if it went well and yet I had my reservations about him. To me, he seemed like a typical ex-copper.

I was introduced to the shop floor manager, the stock controller, a few of the warehouse pickers and the forklift crew on my first day. They all seemed OK. I got stuck in and soon seemed to be accepted by my new workmates, I was introduced to the union representative, who tried to encourage me to get involved on that side of things. I knew that if they were to ever find out what I was really doing, it could end with devastating consequences for me personally. Every Friday I briefed the security manager. He picked me up about a mile away from the warehouse and we would drive out of the city and have a beer, when I'd bring him up to date with names and thieving. No notes were ever taken.

At one of my briefings, the security manager asked if I fancied going to his house. He and his wife were having a few old colleagues and friends around for drinks, mostly other security people and a few ex-police mates. I thought it might be quite useful and it would be good to get out and about. We decided to hold our next debrief at his place and I would stay the night. I was impressed to see that he owned an amazing country cottage with masses of character. It must have been worth a fortune. We took our beers to his home office – another superb set-up. No sooner had I started to give him the details of what had gone on that week when we were interrupted by his wife. He apologised and followed her to the kitchen, leaving me to take in paperwork on his desk. I was shocked to see an invoice from Robson's company for the provision of my services. The bastard was charging them two thousand pounds a week for having me there! I said nothing when my host reappeared and we continued with our regular debrief.

I had become good friends with the factory gang and told the security manager that I had, in fact, joined in with thieving myself in order to be accepted – all of my co-workers were at it in some way. He agreed with this as a workable plan, only reminding me not to encourage anyone, which could be seen as entrapment in any future court case and might result in charges being thrown out. I assured him that they were at it under their own steam. We continued with our drinks until the other guests arrived in the main part of the house. It was great to be offered decent sandwiches and tasty nibbles – and certainly made a welcome change from my regular nightly bag of chips!

I chatted to ex-Avon and Somerset CID police officers, all now retired and involved in the security industry in some way – providing uniformed guarding, surveillance or insurance investigation services. These were typical avenues that ex-coppers commonly took after they left service. They were aware I was working for Robson and it appeared that they had very little respect for him; he was widely known to be a bit of a chancer and scallywag. I did not want to get embroiled in the subject, particularly after I had found out about the invoicing, but I listened without comment as one of them came out with an absolute stinger. He asked me if I knew whether or not Robson still had the contract for a Victorian house near Temple Meads station. I said I was aware of the place but didn't let on that I was actually living there myself. The bloke said that Robson had won a contract to supply security for the building and had guards employed twenty-four hours a day to prevent squatters moving in. I was dumbfounded. The bastard was actually receiving a sizeable amount of money for us living in the place. I was getting a very vivid picture of him as a money-grabbing lowlife. But there was nothing I could do or say about it. I had no choice but to keep quiet.

When I later checked in with Robson, he said I was doing a great job and it was all going really well as far as the security manager was concerned. Everyone was really happy about my reporting. I asked him if there were any signs of an increase in the consultancy fee – without revealing what I knew about the true fee he received – and he reiterated that they were still barely making a profit, but he would let me know if things were to change. He was just a lying bastard.

I needed a way out and it came via a phone call with an old friend. My parents, who knew nothing of my predicament, told me that a Carl Jones had been in touch with them and wanted to know where he could find me. Carl had been on the same 14 INT selection as me, as well as serving some years in the SAS and had previously served in a Royal Armoured Corps regiment. The pair of us had a lot in common. He was a really good bloke and we had got along fine both operationally and socially, sharing a room at the training establishment.

That rapport was re-established the moment we spoke. He asked where the hell I was – he had been trying to track me down for ages. He had teamed up with an ex-Special Branch officer to run a security and investigation company in the upmarket area of Mayfair, London. He told me he had a number of decent jobs on the go and there was an opening if I wanted it. I explained briefly what had been going on over the past year or so and he said, 'Well, get your arse up here, mate, it's time to change things'. I could turn up at their office any time and we would sort everything out from there. I considered briefly before deciding, nothing ventured, nothing gained.

I had a very good idea of how I was going to leave my current position, given the way I had been treated, but I also knew I had to be very careful about how I went about it. If it went wrong I would be in deep shit. First, I asked if I could have a private chat with the union representative – we had become reasonably friendly and he considered me to be a good bloke. I suggested that we nip outside for a cigarette break, getting him away from the rest of our colleagues. He lit up and looked at me in an inquiring way.

I said, 'After I've told you what I'm about to tell you, I need your solemn promise that you do nothing for the next fifteen minutes.'

He looked at me even more quizzically but agreed.

I explained exactly what I had been doing at the warehouse and his face went red. He said that he would keep to his word, but I now had fourteen minutes to get out of there.

As I headed back to the squat I mused that, yes, it was vindictive, but Robson had been lying to me the whole time. I knew he would lose the lucrative contract and that was the idea. I grabbed my stuff from the squat and the lost property office and thumbed lifts to the M4. I was surprised how easy it was to get to the outskirts of London, where I took the underground to Green Park station. Mayfair was a short walk down Piccadilly and through White Horse Street. I checked the cash point machines on the way – you just never knew.

Carl's office was all leather Chesterfield furniture, wooden panels, a very upmarket set-up just around the corner from the Saudi Arabian embassy and less than a fifty-yard walk to the MI5 building that was then on Curzon Street. I was back in the world of spies again. Carl and I went for a beer and a catch-up. He told me that I could live in the spare bedroom at his house in Hertfordshire, he had a second car I could use, and he would put a thousand pounds in my bank account the following day to get me up and running. He could pay me two hundred and fifty pounds a day. He grinned, 'So, you fancy some skulduggery again, then?' I was definitely up for it.

In one of the Shepherd Market pubs in Mayfair, I met an old contact of Carl's. Doug was a one-time mercenary who had fought in Angola alongside the self-styled Colonel Callan, the infamous Costas Georgiou, who had previously been a corporal in the British army's Parachute Regiment and had been executed in 1976. Doug had uses for my surveillance skills and Carl was quite happy for me to be paid directly. At a meeting the following day, I was briefed on what, on the surface, appeared to be a straightforward follow. A lorry at Dover was due to go directly to a container yard in south London. My task was to pick up the lorry as it drove along the A2. I was to get a description of the driver and any passengers. I was to make a note of any stops and get some images. All really quite run-of-the-mill surveillance. I headed off to Kent and plotted up.

About two hours later my target lorry drove past and I tagged on behind it. It was a really easy follow, and I noted all the details of the container yard where the lorry ended up, no stops. I met with Doug the following day and he paid me in cash for the job and asked if I could do the same tasking every week for the following month.

Our next meeting, some weeks later, was at a pub just off the M25 in the Epping area. Doug was with some seven other blokes, all pretty dodgy-looking, to say the least. Doug revealed their intention to intercept the lorry on its journey, remove the driver and take the vehicle to a location where they would empty the load. I got Doug on his own and told him I was not interested. He was disappointed and promised a large share of the profits from the heist. As the papers say, I made my excuses and left. I never heard if they went ahead with the robbery.

The majority of my surveillance work was far more mundane, with some exceptions. A private client asked me to carry out a job in Eltham. He told me that a female would be arriving in a minibus at a particular address, she would go in and pick up a bag and then leave within a few minutes. My task was to follow her and meet him afterwards in a pub in Swiss Cottage to let him know where she ended up. He gave me a description of my target, who would be easy to spot, with pink hair, half shaven in a punk cut.

I found the address and carried out a drive-past. I then parked up to observe the female. After about half an hour of waiting, two police cars arrived in the road, blocking off the road at two ends. Three armed-response officers got out of the vehicles and took up position. About two or three minutes later the minibus arrived, the pink-haired woman jumped out, accompanied by more police officers, and entered the house. Within a few minutes all had returned and driven off, followed by the armed team. I stayed exactly where I was for about fifteen minutes and then drove towards north London and the famous Swiss Cottage pub that gave the area its name.

I told my contact what had happened. He went mad at the fact that I had not got our target's drop-off address, and I told him that I was never going to follow a Met armed-response unit. He was indeed crazy. I never saw him again but found out later that the woman had half of her hair shaven off because my client had hit her with a machete, she had to have loads of stitches and had been taken to a refuge for her own safety. He was later convicted of possession of illegal firearms. I decided that in the future I would ask for fuller briefings.

I continued to do a reasonable amount of work for Carl and was in his office when he received a phone call from a journalist called Luke Jennings, who wanted to be taught how to do surveillance. In return his paper were happy to pay a decent fee and on top of this Luke would write an article about the company and his training. He turned out to be a nice enough guy and we spent three days together, me showing him how I worked and getting him to go through the motions of being an operative, me giving him briefings. Years later a massively successful television series, *Killing Eve*, was made around a book he would write, *Villanelle*. The story followed an eastern bloc female assassin who becomes besotted with the intelligence officer who is hunting her down. I'd never heard of the book before I saw the TV show. There were a few surveillance sequences in the series and I remarked to my wife that, for a change, they were pretty good and quite authentic. Then I saw the book and Luke Jennings's name in the credits. Enough said.

THREE

Carl asked if I was interested in doing a 'babysitting' job for him. A VIP had been working with another team which required more manpower cover to ensure his safety on a twenty-four-hour basis. I was definitely up for it and was at the Mayfair office first thing in the morning with overnight kit and clothes to last about a week.

James Ogilvie-Grant, Viscount Reidhaven was the son of the Earl of Seafield, one of the biggest landowners in Scotland, with an estate of over 180,000 acres in Banffshire. Ogilvie-Grant was also the heir to a fortune which was estimated at being in excess of forty million pounds. Over a period of time he had become involved with a character called Mohammed Iqbal Ali, a Sufi Muslim cult leader. Ali had, over some months, been milking the viscount's funds and had slowly but surely been brainwashing him to such an extent that there were offers of highly lucrative jobs as well as expensive gifts and presents being lavished on both Ali and other cult leaders, all paid for by Ogilvie-Grant. Ali was now controlling the viscount, but his father was having none of it.

A meeting to plan the viscount's rescue was held at the Mayfair office with Lord Seafield, Canadian private detective, Jack Cook, Carl and his business partner, Harry Woods. Harry had previously been a police officer and Special Branch detective.

Cook had experience with similar cults in the USA and Canada. The resulting operation resembled a James Bond plot and the earl confirmed that costs were not an issue to make it work; anything to extract his son from the cult and ensure the viscount's safety and ultimate return to normal and rational thinking, far away from Ali and his followers.

Jack Cook attended Ali's meetings for a few months. He became a regular feature of the cult, establishing his 'legend' as an extremely wealthy visitor to the UK with an interest in Sufism. He made contact with Ogilvie-Grant and reported back to Mayfair on the viscount's state of mind and general demeanour. Cook slowly gained the trust of Ali and his entourage until, eventually, he was accepted and welcomed as a member of the sect. Ali became very friendly, undoubtedly a result of Cook's carefully crafted picture of his own great affluence. The 'sting' was readied. We just needed to get Ali out of the way.

Cook told the cult that he was taking a trip to New York to do some financial business and that he might be away for a number of weeks. He hoped, he said, that Ali and his followers would welcome him back on his return. Ali was interested. He said he had never been to New York and was intrigued by Cook's talk of business. The bait had been taken. Cook duly invited Ali to accompany him to the US, promising they would travel by Concorde and stay at a five-star hotel overlooking Central Park. Ali could not resist and agreed instantly. He had been hooked by his greed, his love of the good things in life – always obtained, of course, at someone else's expense.

A Mercedes stretch limousine arrived at Mohammad Iqbal Ali's home in north London and the 'chauffeur' (ex-SAS) knocked politely at his door, while Jack Cook waited in the vehicle to greet his guest. The chauffeur carried Ali's luggage and opened the back door for him. They drove to Heathrow airport, arriving at the exclusive Concorde departure lounge. In an hour or so, they would be on their way to New York. The chauffeur waited at the terminal to ensure that both Cook and Ali had boarded the flight, before calling Carl in Mayfair. 'They've gone.' Carl thanked him and replaced the receiver. The next phase was to begin.

While Jack had been embedding himself in the cult, other members of the company organised the next part of the operation. Spare keys for Viscount Reidhaven's Chelsea mansion were obtained, two plain but extremely powerful cars were hired and a helicopter was on standby at a private airfield on the outskirts of London. A mansion on the Knoydart peninsula in Scotland was requisitioned and staffed and the local ferryman had been briefed and given an envelope stuffed with cash to ensure his loyalty. He was to tell us should he become aware of any suspicious passengers trying to get to the area and he was, in particular, to let us know immediately should any journalists make inquiries. A bonus had also been given to the local pub landlord for the same thing. The local police sergeant was a relative of one of the team and he guaranteed he would pass on intelligence. A specialist psychiatrist and assistant with a background in de-programming people who had been brainwashed in cult situations had been flown in from the States. Everyone was in place for the next stage.

Jack Cook arrived back in the office; he smiled at Carl and confirmed that Mohammad Ali would be having a bit of a sticky time. Jack had left Ali stranded almost as soon as they arrived, catching the next Concorde to the UK. Ali now had no money, no return flight, no hotel booking and, most importantly, no passport. The sting had worked perfectly; Jack had completed his part of the job. Ali would have to spend a long time explaining his situation to the US authorities and as he was on a Special Branch watch list his visit to New York would last longer than he had envisaged.

The two cars were dispatched to the viscount's place in Chelsea. The first contained two ex-SAS operatives and Harry Woods drove the other, with Carl as the passenger. He sported a luxurious kaftan, a ceremonial turban and had been cultivating a thick black beard for just this moment. Carl, greeted by James Ogilvie-Grant, said he had been sent by Mohammad Ali to ensure his safety and well-being. The viscount was calm and entirely taken in by the set-up. The helicopter, meanwhile, was warming up and the pilot and co-pilot were going through their pre-flight checks as the two cars sped up to the landing pad. The viscount was flown to Fort William in Scotland.

After a few weeks of rest and recuperation out on a private estate, it was time to take James to London to continue his therapy. This was where I came in.

I was to be part of a protection team for James that ensured no unauthorised people were to get near him. It was assumed that Mohammad Iqbal Ali, who had returned to the UK by the time I started, would attempt to contact him. The press was always going to be a problem for such a high-profile figure. Otherwise, the Earl of Seafield allowed certain family members access and James himself was permitted to go for walks outside. We accompanied him at a discreet distance, keeping close enough to react to an emergency situation. Mostly, though, he tended to sit in his room and quite often would be heard quietly chanting to himself – still under the grip of the cult.

The Charter Nightingale was a fantastic facility but was full of sadness, populated by substance abusers and people with eating disorders. I had only ever seen an anorexic person on television before, but there were plenty of them in this place and it really was a pretty awful sight. One time, I was wandering through the main entrance when there was a massive commotion. A teenage American lad had been brought into the hospital by his parents; they were trying to get him to see a medical professional. He claimed to be Jesus and they had tracked him down to a house in Manchester where he had accrued bills on his father's credit cards. A hospital administrator was filling in the boy's entry forms, one of the porters left the front door open and, in a flash, the lad was gone and was legging it down the road.

Harry Woods walked in just after this had happened and spoke to the parents. It turned out that they were a massively wealthy family and owned a big communications company that supplied the US military. Harry did an immediate sales–pitch and we were tasked with trying to recover the lad. I finished my shift and Harry asked me if I was free to go to the house in Manchester where the boy would return and try to talk him into coming back to London. After all, I was a trained handler and negotiator. I saw no problem with at least giving it a go. Jack Cook and I drove up that evening and the following day we went to the address where he had been living since the family came over from the US and he had dropped out of university.

Jack and I approached the house, where a few teenagers were gathered in the hallway, all of them peaceful and quite welcoming. We were allowed to go into the living room to meet the lad, who had about ten or twelve other teenagers sat around on the floor in front of him. It turned out that not only did he think he was Jesus, they did as well! We asked him for a private word but were told that we could openly talk in front of his 'disciples'– they were quite enchanting, in a strange sort of way. I couldn't work out if they were drugged up or just extremely relaxed, but it meant they did not pose a problem.

We tried to negotiate our target back to London with us. He refused, but passively, and as he did so, one or two of the girls at the house started crying; it was a surreal scene. A few of his followers now moved to position themselves between the two of us and their leader. There was no way that we were going to be able to talk him out and it would now appear that to physically remove him was going to prove impossible so we said our farewells. The group's demeanour remained calm and they thanked us for visiting them and said we could call back and join them any time. We returned to London and told the parents what had happened. They pretty much resolved on the spot to head back to the USA, saying they intended to cut off the lad's financial support. We never heard from them or their son again.

I decided to go to breakfast in the canteen one morning and walked into the lift to see I was sharing the space with a small, thin man with dark, sunken eyes and a rather attractive tall, slim lady with blonde hair. Both were immaculately dressed; he was wearing a very upmarket, chalk-stripe suit and silk tie and she was wearing what was obviously a mink, full-length coat and lots of very expensive jewellery. Bit over the top for breakfast.

The man asked if I was looking after James and said that he knew the family. He seemed quite knowledgeable and for a moment I wondered if they were there to extract information but it soon became evident that they had their own conditions and just happened to know about the viscount situation. Both had been heavy cocaine users, had a nasty session and booked themselves into the rehabilitation programme. They knew that they had problems and they knew that they did not have to be there, but they were both volunteering to try and clean up their act. When I said I worked for an exclusive security and investigation company in Mayfair, he immediately said, 'Harry Wood's firm': he had seen Ogilvie-Grant and had also clocked Harry the previous day and had put two and two together. It turned out that he and Harry had been at school together, but it had also been a few years since they had met. He asked if I would arrange a meeting at the hospital as there was a good possibility that they would be requiring our services.

This was my first encounter with Guido Hughes and Leonora Watkins, an unlikely couple. He was the son of a wealthy socialite family, his father a character called Billy Hughes who was a great friend of Princess Margaret. Leonora was the estranged wife of Michael Watkins, a London businessman who had been jailed for fraud cases involving share 'ramping' (manipulating prices for their own benefit). Their orbit had taken in the same exclusive nightclubs and glitzy restaurants, where they found that they both shared similar tastes – one being cocaine. Hughes said he was an executive film producer and movie industry financier. A totally separate Hollywood film producer and director had the same name, which must surely have secured client meetings for the London Hughes. He never denied being his namesake at the meetings I attended with him and appeared to have made a lucrative career from so doing.

Harry duly met with the couple and asked if I would be happy to leave Viscount Reidhaven and provide Hughes and Watkins's private security. Ogilvie-Grant would only require one live-in bodyguard and a full-time nurse and cook who would double up as housekeeper. They would be in Kent and, as I was still based in Hertfordshire, it seemed better that I switch teams. Both Hughes and Watkins had their concerns; Guido told me that he had heard on the grapevine about threats to have his legs broken. How much of that was banter I did not know, but they both seemed very worried.

In my new role I was to work alongside two ex-SAS guys. We had rooms in a smart hotel on the Bayswater Road around the corner from the apartment shared by Guido and Leonora. They were both quite happy for us to make sure they were locked up safe and sound at night. There was never a specific time to meet and pick up each day; we were alerted by phone about thirty minutes before we were needed. We worked a shift pattern between the three of us and everything ticked along quite happily.

The couple had an underground lock-up containing a spruced-up BMW 5 Series, a brand-spanking-new Daimler Jaguar and an Aston Martin DB6. We were allowed to use the BMW and the Jaguar ourselves but, no matter how many times I begged, Hughes would never let me take the DB6 home! The strange thing, though, as Guido admitted to me one day, was that he could not drive and had no plans to learn. The pair travelled everywhere by chauffeur-driven Rolls-Royce. He explained that, when he was young, he had been told by a gypsy that he would die behind the wheel of a car. That had left him totally paranoid and unwilling to drive himself, even though he owned those magnificent vehicles.

Both of them loved the London social scene and I have to admit we always had the best table booked for dinner and ate in some fantastic places. They knew a number of celebrities and would always introduce us to their friends as if we were really part of their set-up and close friends of theirs. I got to meet such acting luminaries of the time as Dennis Waterman and his then-wife Rula Lenska and Susan George and her husband Simon MacCorkindale. On each occasion Guido would encourage us to stick very close and become part of the conversation and be his friend rather than his security detail.

At a celebrity fundraiser one evening at the Dorchester hotel, a socialite friend of Guido's family, Roddy Llewellyn, made his way over to speak to us. He looked at me and said, 'We have met before, I believe?' We had but I was amazed he had remembered. Our previous encounter went way back to my selection process for 14 INT, when those involved were not allowed to drink or socialise in Hereford and had to find other watering holes. A few of us frequented an upmarket bar and restaurant just outside Abergavenny called the Walnut Tree. This had been Roddy's local too – he was the baronet of Llewllyn from nearby Aberdare – and we chatted a few times. I was impressed that he had remembered me from those days and was quite aware of what my role was now – he was a very astute man. Before he moved on that night, he took me aside and asked me to really look after Guido. He said he knew he had some serious problems, although I wasn't sure and didn't ask if he meant the substance abuse or the alleged physical threats.

Guido and Leanora spent the night with some friends in Wimbledon on another occasion and asked if Trak, my Fijian ex-SAS partner that day, and I could pick them up late the following morning. I took our driving duties – out of Bayswater, down to Sloane Square and across the Albert Bridge towards Wandsworth. As we turned into the high street, we noticed a police officer sprinting around a large rubbish skip outside a pub in pursuit of a bloke who had obviously stolen his radio. The culprit was being egged on by two or three others and the policeman was having a seriously hard time. I drove on for about another fifty metres and then Trak and I just looked at each other.

'Reckon we ought to go back, then?' he said.

I looked back and said, 'Yep, reckon we should.'

I spun the Jaguar around and we headed back to find the policeman in a tussle and being dragged to the ground by two men with another two of their friends looking like they were about to join in. Trak and I jumped out of the car and ran over. Trak dragged the assailants off the police officer and, when one of the other men moved towards us in a seriously threatening way, I smashed the heel of my palm into his mouth and he dropped like a brick, gurgling, spluttering and bleeding from his mouth, I had cracked his false teeth open and now the bloke was choking. I got on top of him and pinned him down. He moaned and groaned and was in a right old state. He was either drunk or on drugs – all of them were.

In the distance I could hear sirens, heading our way from different directions. The policeman had managed to make an officer-in-distress call and the cavalry was riding to his rescue.

I looked at the copper and said, 'Make fucking sure you tell them who the good guys are.' I envisaged the two of us being included in a kicking from his backup.

The support arrived, about twelve of them in different vehicles and the officer pointed us out immediately and said that we were assisting him. Thank God for that: last thing I needed was a battering from a police truncheon or a face full of CS gas.

We left the police to sort out the idiots who had been causing the problem and Trak and I made a casual but swift exit. Without saying it out loud, we knew that we had done our good deed for the day and, nodding towards the Jaguar, we did not want to get bogged down with making statements and possibly having to attend court. After picking Guido and Leanora up I drove back via Putney, giving Wandsworth High Street a wide berth, just in case.

Our time with Guido and Leanora was more usually relaxed, more so than on most close protection jobs, when you'd have to wear a suit and tie. Guido actively asked us to dress down and just look casual and the assignments were pretty sweet too. We got to travel to Dublin on a few occasions, as Guido had family connections and I escorted Leanora to Cyprus to visit some old friends, marking the first time I had ever flown first class. I hardly had to do anything – after seeing her safely to her destination in the resort of Ayia Napa, I had time to visit my brother and his family in Nicosia, where he worked with the United Nations. It was a nice little trip at the client's expense.

I had been in Cyprus some years previously, also serving with the UN peacekeeping force and knew the region reasonably well. Not far from the UN's quarters at the Ledra Palace hotel, Nicosia, you could cross the border into northern Cyprus, in an area known as 'Turkey Town', a great place to acquire counterfeit goods. I managed to get a Rolex Submariner watch, a great pair of Ray-Ban Aviators and a load of Ralph Lauren shirts and T-shirts, all for less than a quarter of what I would pay for the genuine article back home. I flew back two days later on my own, again first class and, as I was not on duty, I indulged myself with the copious amounts of the Moët & Chandon on offer. Very nice it was too. The job only came to an end after Guido and Leonora split up and Guido no longer thought he was at risk. Nevertheless, it had been a good run and I had enjoyed myself. I went home and waited for the next call from Carl and Harry.

Following the success in extracting James Ogilvie-Grant and ensuring his subsequent protection, the company began to be used by a number of cult deprogrammers and psychiatrists. It cost a fortune to stage such operations and the service really was limited to a clique of wealthy families. One such person was the mother of a twenty-eight-year-old US citizen who was living in London, Mary Ryan. She had gained a good position working for a Japanese company after attending Harvard University. For a short time, she had worked at the White House under President Reagan, before extending her qualifications at the London School of Economics and eventually she had been offered a computer consultancy role in a company based in north London. She shared a house in Notting Hill with a fellow employee, a Japanese girl who was a consultant at the same company.

Carl and Harry were approached by a solicitor acting on behalf of Mary's mother, Deborah Ryan. She was convinced that her daughter was involved with a Japanese cult and said that Mary had become estranged from her after moving in with her housemate. She had suggested seeing a psychiatrist, but her daughter had rejected the idea and they had become even more distant. This had only deepened Deborah's suspicions.

A plan was formulated along the lines of that which had been used to free Viscount Reidhaven. Mary would be taken by car to a deprogrammer in a rural mansion house. Jack Cook and an ex-mercenary friend of Carl's, Danny Thomas, would drive the front car and would ensure that there were no problems. The second car would be driven by me disguised as a chauffeur. Mary's aunt – who was in on the scheme – would phone her niece and ask her to dinner at a Heathrow hotel, on the pretext that she was just passing through Europe on her way back to the States after a holiday. She would offer to send a car, which would be my vehicle. The allegations raised by Mary's mother went unchecked as the operation swung into action.

Ryan and Harry were in my car and, as we drove towards Notting Hill, Mary's aunt made her call. I dropped my two passengers about fifty metres away from the house and the front car went on ahead. I pulled up at the target, donned my chauffeur's hat and knocked at the door. Mary said she would be out in a few minutes and as she went back inside, I spotted her Japanese housemate in the corridor. The two of them were obviously confused as to why her aunt had set up this impromptu dinner. I heard Mary say she believed it was strange and out of character, but she came anyway.

When we were ready to set off, I asked if it was OK for me to let my office know that my passenger had been picked up safe and sound. She agreed. In fact, I was calling Jack in the lead car and giving Deborah and Harry time to walk up behind us, jump in either side of Mary and box her in – not surprisingly, the daughter went bonkers. Harry had a blanket that he quickly wrapped around her arms as she kicked and punched out like crazy, landing some serious blows on her mother.

We had rented a luxurious mansion in extensive grounds with electronic gates and high walls that protected the house from being overlooked. Ready to meet us were two Americans – a psychiatrist and her medical colleague – along with Mary's aunt and a number of security staff in civilian clothing, who all actually had special forces backgrounds. Harry and Deborah managed to get Mary into the house, assisted by the aunt. She was then taken off to be assessed by the mental health team. We gathered outside to establish a security rota. I was not due to start my shift till the following morning and headed home.

The electronic security gates were already wide open when I returned. Strange. As I approached the house itself I could see a few of the security team milling around the main door, talking to Harry. I spotted Mary herself wandering down the path to the main gates and stopped the car immediately. I asked her where she was going and she replied, 'Better speak to your boss,' and left the grounds. This was getting stranger.

Harry greeted me just as Jack Cook drove up. 'The shit has hit the fan, big style,' Harry said, looking visibly shook up. During the de-programming session that had lasted much of the previous night it had been proved that Mary was not under any kind of external control; she was an intelligent woman who could make her own mind up about what she was doing with her life. More shocking yet, and this was the crunch, she thought that her mother, our client, herself had serious mental welfare issues. Our target, Mary, was in reality concerned about her mother's state of mind.

I looked at both of my colleagues and said I was going to return the hire car, get my own vehicle back and make my way home. I didn't fancy being around when the police turned up – which was likely any time now. Surely Mary would be making contact with them even as we spoke?

I phoned Carl and asked him to get in touch as soon as any new operation was available. I hadn't heard anything after a week or so and decided to remind Carl and Harry who I was. When I was nearly at the office, in Shepherd Market, I rang ahead to see if anyone wanted a coffee brought up. Carl was not only not in the mood for a hot drink, he told me not to come to the office at all: CID officers from Reading were in the process of arresting Harry for kidnap and were looking for the other people involved in the job. The description of the driver that they had got from Mary Ryan had led them to believe it was Carl but they were not one hundred percent sure and after brief questioning he had been left alone. Harry, on the other hand, was in the deep, smelly area and was taken to West End Central police station for questioning. Being an ex-copper himself, he knew the score and spent the next six hours repeating, 'No comment.'

Harry and Deborah were facing charges of kidnap in the high court and, separately, Deborah was charged with holding her daughter against her will. This was looking very serious and could have easily ended up with custodial sentences. I was still quite amazed that the police had not pursued me as the driver as I suppose I was as blameworthy as the other two but, somehow, I was not arrested. A deal was offered: the trial would be dropped if Deborah was to agree to an injunction being taken out against her. This prevented Ryan from contacting her daughter for the rest of her life; never again – this was for ever. She agreed and the case against Harry was also dropped. Deborah Ryan headed back to America still of the opinion that what she did was out of motherly love. She genuinely had concerns for Mary's welfare and considered that she had done the right thing.

FOUR

I had been working as a self-employed freelance investigator and surveillance operative for a number of different companies, and I had also joined teams with other people who worked what was referred to as 'the circuit'. I had become quite well known in this market and because of my background, previous training and operational experience I was never short of offers of work. One such task I was asked to run was to turn out to be quite a shocker.

'Papa, this is Mike, over.' My radio burst into life. 'There is a plod car making its way up the road, I think he is looking for you, over.' Very funny, I thought, my team motorbike man was obviously bored to tears, but then we had been sat in the same spot on the same road in Birmingham watching a travel agency for three days.

We had been tasked with a straightforward matrimonial surveillance job: the wife of the agency's manager was curious to know who he was meeting in his lunch breaks and why he had suddenly started staying at hotels after various conferences, when he would normally have gone home. Unfortunately for Mark, searching for the answers involved a lot of hanging about and there was no way around that. I got on the radio to say that if he wanted to relieve his boredom he could go for a ride around the area and Annie, my other team member, and I would keep the target covered. I soon realised Mark hadn't actually been joking.

A Heckler & Koch machine pistol pointed at my head from the direction of the right-hand side of the car and a Glock semi-automatic pistol appeared in front. Three police cars had blocked us in and an armed response unit was surrounding us. I put my hands on the windscreen and shouted at Annie to do the same.

I had been smoking a cigarette shortly before and my window was still open. The nearest armed officer moved closer and told me to open the door and get out with my hands fully in the air. I told him that I was not taking my hands off the windscreen and that he could open the door. He shouted the same order again and again I shouted back at him that I was not letting my hands go out of sight to open the door.

One of his colleagues, also armed with a Glock, moved forward and opened my door. There was no way that I was going to drop my hands. I told Annie to do the same and not let her hands drop out of sight of the coppers.

We both then got out and placed our arms on the roof, stretching them across as far as we could. Both of us were searched quite unceremoniously, right in the middle of a busy shopping street. It was all pretty horrendous. I was questioned forcefully about what we were up to and explained everything. The armed response team were stood down and two CID officers continued to question us separately. Luckily, our stories corroborated one another and the police were satisfied.

I was asked to open the boot of the car to reveal three overnight bags, camera equipment and radio-charging sets. I explained we were finishing the job that afternoon and heading straight home at end of play. One of the bags belonged to Mark and I didn't know what was in it. The officer was annoyed all over again when he realised there was another person involved in our enterprise – I'd forgotten about the motorbike man. I called him up and a few minutes later Mark's bike pulled up beside us. He was grinning from ear to ear.

An armed robbery had taken place at a jewellery shop about ten days previously and a traffic warden whose route took him up our street every day had reported our presence. The suspects in the robbery were, like Annie and me, one male and a female, and they'd got away in a black VW Golf. The shop was about fifty metres away from where we had been plotting up – me and Annie, sat together, in – you've guessed it – a black VW Golf. You could not make it up.

The CID officers continued their search of my vehicle and contacted our employers to get us the all-clear. Everyone relaxed. One former motorbike traffic officer admired Mark's sharp bike and asked what it could do. Quick as a flash, Mark responded that it did seventy miles an hour on the motorway and thirty miles an hour in built-up areas. The officer grinned and said, 'Smart arse.'

While all this had been going on, armed police, CID and passers-by watching the whole thing unfold, I had been keeping an eye on our target, who was at his desk on the first-floor office at the travel agency. By some strange quirk, he appeared to have been blissfully unaware of the scenario unfolding up the road. I decided that we may as well hang around to finish the job and, that way, we could at least let the client know the full results of our surveillance, right up to the end. Eventually the subject packed up, locked his office and drove home. Over the days that we had been watching he had not met anyone in his lunch break and had gone straight home at the end of every day. It had, nevertheless, been a job to remember, even though it hadn't quite gone as planned.

The mix-up with the police didn't seem to cause me any problems with the agency who'd employed me. A few days later they asked if I could go to their London office the next day for a full brief on a new task. On the surface, this appeared to be quite straightforward surveillance of a man who lived in Phillimore Gardens, just a short distance from Kensington High Street. Our client had been approached by the subject to enter into a business agreement and we were to assist with due diligence. I was told by Peter, the agency boss, that I could employ whatever manpower I needed as the client was very wealthy and wanted twenty-four-hour coverage. This was a very rare request.

My daytime team consisted of a covert van, two cars with a single male in one and a male and female in the other and, as that part of London could get very clogged with traffic, I added two motorbikes. At night, I needed only a covert van and a single car with a male and female. I had to be available myself twenty-four hours a day to answer any questions the client might have. I was on a really good rate of pay and was happy to comply, telling the night team that if there was any movement or activity at all then I was to be briefed immediately.

We were plotted up at the target's house for three days before he finally emerged. His description and that of his wife was exactly as we'd been briefed they would be. Video footage and photographs were taken by the operator in the covert van. The subject and his wife took a maroon Mercedes estate car along Kensington High Street, turning right onto Brompton Road and then left into Hans Road, a street bordering Harrods, where he parked up. All the team had now seen and identified the subject and I told the covert van operator to remain at the home address.

The client rang at that moment. This was the first I'd heard from him since we started: 'Where is he? What is he doing? Who is he with?' Rather strange, I thought – as soon as the subject was on the move, he phoned. I briefed that the subject and his wife were in the food hall in Harrods. I was asked to call him back as soon as they came out of Harrods and to give a running commentary of their movements.

After about an hour the subject and his wife drove away home using the same roads as before. As soon as their destination became obvious I told the following team to hold back and the covert van operator to let us know when they were in his sight.

The motorbikes would have easily caught up with them along Kensington High Street if they had gone anywhere else and now I could stand them down too.

'That is bravo one and bravo two now at alpha one,' reported the van operator, confirming they were both back at Phillimore Gardens.

I briefed the client. He said we could all stand down for a while as he did not think that the target would be going anywhere for the rest of the day. Again, I was slightly bemused by what turned out to be his accurate forecasting of our target's movements. I was beginning to get the distinct impression that all was not quite what it seemed, and so it transpired, although it would take a while for the whole picture to be revealed.

The following day, around eleven in the morning, the subject's wife left the property and got into a taxi. We let her run as she was of no real interest to us or the client. We continued to plot up, cover the area and wait for the subject to make a show. At around half past twelve he came out of his front door, got into the Mercedes, took the same route as the previous day and again ended up in Hans Road. I rang the client, who went into meltdown, firing questions at me again.

'Where is he now? What door did he use at Harrods? Can you see him?' He sounded quite anxious, to say the least.

I kept talking and told him every movement that the subject was making, as it happened. He walked out of the rear doors at Harrods and took a route that would eventually lead him along Hans Crescent and on to Sloane Street where he headed north and wandered into another famous department store, Harvey Nichols, at the very top of the road. My male and female operatives covered his movements inside the store, appearing to amble around casually while the bikes and I secured and covered all exit routes. At length the target strolled back to his car in Hans Road and drove home.

At every stage of the unremarkable shopping excursion, I had to keep the client, who I now knew to be named George, informed of the exact location. George was more than interested to see if our man had spoken to anyone, what he had in the way of shopping, what he was wearing and every other detail, no matter how small. He had begun referring to the target as a Mr Davies which I thought highly unlikely, as the man looked more obviously Saudi Arabian or Lebanese but we used this name for him throughout the rest of the job.

We followed Mr Davies back to his house and, after it was confirmed by the covert van operator that he had entered the property, I told the van to lift off and go and have a break in one of the parks nearby. I would take up his position for a few hours. I called George and let him know the latest details.

I had been parked in Phillimore Gardens for about half an hour when a car containing two men pulled up beside me and the driver indicated that I should open my window, which I did. He looked at me in an inquisitive way and asked if I was 'On board'.

I looked back equally questioningly, 'On board? What is that?'

He said that was OK, there was no problem.

His passenger then leaned across and said, 'Bloody hell – Rob Lewis!'

They parked up behind me and we got out for a chat. The passenger was an old mate of mine from the FRU who had gone on to transfer to MI5 and was running one of their surveillance teams. They coincidentally had a subject they were watching in the same street. We caught up for a while, safe in the knowledge that both of us were far enough away from our respective targets to go unnoticed should either of them look out of their properties. Within ten minutes another vehicle pulled up where we were chatting and a woman passenger motioned to Ernie, my old mate, to come to the car. He had a quick chat with her and then wandered back to me and just said 'Branch'. He meant Special Branch. They also had a target – an entirely separate subject – in Phillimore Gardens. This was unbelievable!

In one unremarkable road, about 150 metres long, there were three surveillance tasks going on, encompassing the security services, Special Branch and our job, which itself was mostly manned by ex-FRU and 14 INT people. I was surprised that my lot were not asked to move out from the area as the others would have tasks that would have been diplomatic- or possibly terrorism-related but they were fine with us staying there.

Peter asked me to take over George, who had been driving him insane with endless late night and early morning calls. It would effectively become my own job. In return, Peter asked that I pay him ten per cent of whatever I earned, an introduction fee. I agreed. I had George's office address in Lowndes Square, a very elegant and expensive area of Knightsbridge. George was an extremely nice bloke; we chatted about the job and he thanked me for the professional way that it was being run. Mr Davies, he said, was going to be going to Cannes in the South of France at the weekend and would be there for about ten days. I did not ask him how he knew this, but listened carefully. Peter would organise flights for three of us to follow him out and stay at the Carlton Intercontinental luxury hotel on the Boulevard de la Croisette. It was all quite amazing.

This was an annual trip for Mr Davies, who would go with his two brothers and their families. They always stayed at the same hotel and would spend a great deal of time gambling at the casino at the Carlton: we were to watch their every move and report back to George as usual. He handed me a bulging brown envelope of cash to cover the previous week's surveillance and some up-front running money for the trip to Cannes. I headed back to Phillimore Gardens and sorted out cash into separate envelopes for the operatives. It was a lot of money for all of us and everyone in the team was more than happy. I chose Mark – the biker who had been cheeky with the former traffic cop – and a female operative, Kim, to accompany me to Cannes in a few days' time. Needless to say, they were more than happy as well.

We flew to Nice and took a taxi for an hour's journey along the spectacular coastline to reach a hotel that was equally stunning, a serious five-star set-up with its own private beach. I rang George to let him know that we were in place and would be ready for Mr Davies' arrival the following day. The team at Phillimore Gardens would see him through to departures at Heathrow and keep us updated every step of the way.

Mr Davies' flight went without a hitch and Mark, Kim and I hung around the front of the hotel to watch for the arrival. The family turned up at the Carlton in a minibus and Davies booked into the hotel with his brothers and their own families. As ever, I updated George. We then spent the next few days enjoying a luxurious working time, as Davies never left the hotel. He spent his days on its beach and the evenings at the casino with his brothers. Their wives seemed to just wander back and forth, Mrs Davies heading into town a few times, arriving back a few hours later laden with shopping. George would call for updates two or three times a day.

George at length asked if I could get near enough to Davies to find out what he was talking about with his brothers at the roulette tables, but when I had been near him before, I explained, the family had spoken Arabic. George suggested my team could play the tables but I knew I didn't have the skill or experience to get away with passing myself off as a seasoned gambler; security was extremely tight. Then he dropped a bombshell, asking me to come to his hotel.

George was in Cannes as well!

My employer's hotel, it turned out, was a mere two hundred metres away in another area of the seafront. I was soon face-to-face with him in his foyer, glancing at him in an inquiring manner but saying nothing about how odd this all was. It seemed to me to be very obvious that there was something about this job that George was not telling me, but I was prepared to wait to find out what was really going on. If he picked up on my suspicions he either didn't let on or didn't care. He had another thickly packed brown envelope that was obviously stuffed with cash and asked if I could play the tables to get close to Davies. I reiterated that I did not know enough about the games to be convincing, softening the blow by adding that the restaurant overlooked the casino and that we had been booking a table there every evening. We had a fantastic view of the whole area: if Davies was there, we could see him at all times. George seemed OK with this solution.

When we returned to London I arranged for the UK team to pick up Davies at Heathrow: they were all available and ready to get back to work. Mark, Kim and I were to follow on later and observed Davies and his party leaving the hotel in their minibus. I updated George and we followed on a later flight.

We settled back into the routine at Phillimore Gardens: Mr Davies would drive to Harrods and Harvey Nichols and George would phone in a panic, demanding to know every last movement. At length, my instincts about there being something off with George's peculiar obsession with the minutiae of his target's life were proved to be correct. The truth came out one day when we followed Davies up Sloane Street, heading as usual, in the direction of Harvey Nichols. George was even more jumpy than usual when I told him. He stayed on the phone and, as we continued up past the Millennium hotel on the western side of Sloane Street, I noticed George himself peeping his head out of the front door of the building, looking north – the direction in which I was just then reporting the subject to be headed. I was on the other side of the road and, although he couldn't see me, I had a good view of both the target and George himself. George dashed out to a taxi, quickly followed by a woman – Mrs Davies. There it was. I wasn't surprised and I said nothing.

George finally confessed what I already knew about a week later. At his Lowndes Square office he explained about the affair with Mrs Davies and wanting to know her husband's movements. The couple's son had also known all about what was going on and was fully supportive of his mother. He wanted her to leave his father, who was apparently a bully, a ruthless character adept at beating both his wife and son. The son would phone George when Davies was leaving the house and George would alert me. George was briefing me on the real situation because things were changing; they were now taking their relationship to the next level. Mrs Davies had agreed to leave her husband and George was going to go back to Lebanon. That meant, of course, that there was no further need for our services. I was gutted. At one point the job had looked like it was never going to end; all the team had earned good money and everybody was disappointed to be told it was over. Now it was my turn to hand over a brown envelope, this time to Peter, with his ten per cent. We continued to work together.

Insurance companies all use private detectives and surveillance teams to watch and film individuals making large claims. It's standard procedure in order to determine if the claims are valid. Peter had some quite big insurance names on his client list and, as I had covert cameras fitted in my car and in bags and I could wear them on my body I was sometimes asked to carry out such investigations. Most of the time they were pretty straightforward and invariably quite mundane but some were ludicrous. People making major claims would be told by their solicitors that they should expect to be watched and not to compromise their actions by doing anything out of the ordinary. However, some people are just stupid.

Along with another inquiry agent, I was once asked to go to Liverpool to carry out surveillance on a man who had brought a million-pound insurance claim against his tyre-fitting company employers. A piece of equipment had been fitted incorrectly, had flown off a machine he worked on and he took the force of the large chunk of metal in the hip. This evidence was not disputed and hospital reports showed that he had suffered quite a bad injury. What was in question were the subsequent claims to having sustained life-changing injuries. He claimed that he could not have sex with his wife, hold his grandchildren, drive, play golf and so on; you name it, the list was endless.

He was to undergo a medical interview prior to the case going to court for the final hearing. Andy – the guy I was working with – and I plotted up at the hospital to see what we could see. We were not to be disappointed. His solicitor had briefed him well and he put on an obvious show, fully aware that he was being observed. He was lifted out of his car by two or three members of his family and into a wheelchair, one of his party wrapping a shawl around him and helping him inside the hospital. When they left the same drama unfolded, as they battled to get him back into the car.

The following day Andy and I had to keep an eye on his home address and it wasn't easy. Residents on his estate were very observant and surveillance-aware. We weren't readily able to stay in one place. While I did my best, Andy went to park by the local estate sports hall. He was soon in contact.

'Mate, you are not going to believe what I am looking at,' he said, almost unable to control his laughter.

Our target had kept on his position as a martial arts instructor and was still running regular sessions in the hall. I could not believe it. Andy had seen his poster, the man holding a high-kicking pose, encouraging local people to attend his lessons. The times and dates were all up there. Too good to be true. Even better, our subject himself was soon in sight – plain sight. He came out of his home for all to see, in his front garden, hanging out with some friends or perhaps potential students. He was demonstrating one-armed press ups. I managed to capture about twenty minutes of covertly filmed martial arts routines. When he finished we went off to have a beer.

The next evening we plotted up, me at the subject's house and Andy at the sports hall, hoping to film him going from one place to the other. I'd been waiting for some fifteen minutes when the target appeared at the front door, talking on his mobile. He was dressed in a baggy tracksuit and trainers. After a few minutes he turned and spoke to someone inside the property, shut the door and then proceeded to set off at a jog. This was the same bloke who had been seen, thirty-six hours earlier, attending his hospital interview in a wheelchair. Andy started his video to catch our miraculously healed target in the act of running towards him.

The sports hall had a public viewing area from where I filmed the subject using a covert camera in a sports bag. He spent forty minutes teaching his martial arts students and we now had enough to make the client and the insurance company very happy indeed. We decided to leave after forty minutes or so, before there was any chance of compromising ourselves.

When the case reached the high court some months later, Andy and I had to attend in case we were asked to give evidence. The lawyer for the insurance company briefed us on the procedure before, armed with the video footage evidence we had gathered, he approached the claimant's solicitor and asked to speak privately before going into court. He said that the insurance company would be prepared to make an out-of-court settlement: one pound. The lawyer played our video and showed the photographs. The two parties negotiated a settlement that eventually covered just the injury the man had sustained. The final figure they settled on was thirty thousand pounds, a bit of a drop from the million our target had hoped for. He must have been seriously disappointed and I wished that we had worked on a percentage of the money we'd saved the company rather than our usual daily rate. We would have had a seriously nice little earner.

I was to be back in Liverpool not long afterwards. This time it was to join a large team with a difficult and dangerous task. A major company – a household name – was having problems with strikes, orders were being disrupted and the management feared they might go under. They were up against a militant faction of the workforce and management were unable to identify the main antagonists. They had become desperate to weed them out or, at the very least, establish some kind of control over the extent of the disruption they were able to cause. A march to be held the next weekend in support of further strike action was to be our opportunity to bring a halt to the havoc. We had to be particularly professional as the militant members were also quite a nasty looking bunch and it could easily have turned violent should any of our team get compromised. I joined our team at a hotel on the Wirral and met the twelve operators, half of whom I already knew from previous jobs.

The team were split into two, one half positioned along the route of the march in vans or cars with recording set-ups and the rest marching, blending in by posing as strikers. They would get as close to the troublemakers as possible. Team leader Dougie made placards in bright, reflective green to ensure our operatives stood out among the thousand or so workers and their supporters. We would be able to pinpoint our colleagues in the throng.

I had a remote-controlled video camera concealed in the grill of my car and all I had to do was point my car in the direction that I wanted video taken and watch along on the small portable screen in the car. I was sure to switch off the camera's auto-focus, otherwise it would simply have recorded not very useful footage of the car's grill. As it was, it filmed through the gaps and was pretty effective and, best of all, totally unnoticeable to anyone in the crowd.

Our team came away with an excellent result. Dougie showed the video footage and photographs annotated with names – job done. The client was sufficiently impressed to give Dougie some extra funds for the team to have dinner and drinks at the hotel for another night. A very nice gesture – and unprecedented too.

We were soon outside on the hotel terrace, feeling pretty pleased with ourselves. I shared a table with almost all the team and got the chance to meet those I hadn't worked with. We were all ex-forces. Among them was Martin, ex-Grenadier Guards and someone who had also been engaged in what he referred to as 'other special stuff'. When pushed, he admitted that he had been with my old outfit, the FRU. I had never seen him before in my life and it was clear that he had no idea who I was either. I listened but said nothing. He talked about a FRU course he had been on and how he had been a handler involved in recruitment and surveillance. Everyone was impressed. He slipped in a few names – all genuine people and names I had known in reality. Had he, someone else asked, ever come across a former Royal Marine named Mike Kerry? This member of our team had served with Kerry at 42 Commando. Yes, said Martin, they were on the same selection in the FRU and had worked together on numerous tasks.

This was too much. I had shared a house with Kerry in Northern Ireland and we had been part of the same team; he was actually a very close mate. I quietly left the table to find a secluded spot in the hotel bar. I rang Mike to ask if he had ever come across this Martin character. His reply confirmed my suspicions, 'Complete "Walter Mitty", mate. What shit is he coming out with?' The truth, he continued, was that, yes, he and Martin had indeed been on the same selection but the other man had been rejected around week two. He was said to have extreme loyalist tendencies and it was feared he would be biased and, anyway, he verged on the unhinged with an obsession he had for paramilitaries on the loyalist side. He swiftly received a one-way train ticket off the course. The real story revealed, I returned to the table and re-joined the conversation, which was still in full swing, about FRU operations. It was time for me to jump in with my own knowledge of the unit.

'So, Martin,' I asked, 'when were you at the FRU – what years?' He had the correct dates. I replied that I had served for three years with the detachment over the same period and that Mike Kerry and I had lived together and worked on the same team. He blustered some lame story that he had been working on the 'UK side'. It made no sense and he was clearly lying. The sad thing was that he was actually quite a competent operative and a capable man. But that wasn't enough for him. Like so many in our industry he had to make out he was 'special'. He soon departed, red-faced, to his room.

It was not the last time I was to come across a Walter Mitty character. They were always out there, getting jobs with clients based on their made-up stories and false backgrounds.

FIVE

Scappaticci. No matter which side you were on during the Troubles, that name was synonymous with the intrigue, conspiracy and fear of the IRA for the people of Belfast and Northern Ireland.

Freddie Scappaticci was the son of an Italian immigrant family who had settled in Belfast and as a youngster he grew up in the infamous Markets area of the city. This was a tough enough start in life for anyone but he was no ordinary bloke. He was a loyal republican who would go on to rise through the ranks of the IRA due to his ruthlessness. He hated informers with a vengeance and was given the task of running the IRA's internal investigation team; weeding out possible informants involved with Special Branch and military intelligence. His team – nicknamed the 'Nutting Squad' – tortured, maimed and executed those suspected of giving intelligence to the security forces. Scappaticci was interned in the seventies alongside the likes of Gerry Adams and Alex Maskey; this cemented his reputation for being a hardline IRA member and he was held in high esteem as a loyal and trusted republican lieutenant.

After a member of the IRA was arrested and questioned by the RUC, the first person who would speak to them on their release was Scappaticci – often with deadly consequences. The Nutting Squad would set about their grim work, mercilessly ending the lives of people they thought may have been giving over information. Their torture methods included strapping people to gas cookers and turning the heat up slowly and they were known for carrying out 'kneecappings', in which a pistol was aimed behind the victim's knee in order that the bullet would shatter the patella. Targets included not only informers but petty criminals and those who had carried out terrorism without getting permission via the IRA's established chain of command. The Royal Victoria hospital had to become very proficient at treating the many victims of a kneecapping, in addition to patching up those wounded in other kinds of shootings and bombings. When bullets were not available, the punishment squad would use power drills to cause the same effect. Scappaticci would report any information gleaned from terrified victims to the high command of the IRA. Each brutal act further enhanced his already fearsome name.

Scappaticci controlled his squad with an iron fist; everyone feared him. He was known throughout the province by the nickname 'Scap'. But there was a secret side to Scap – he was himself an informant who had for many years been passing intelligence to the security forces and in particular to the FRU. He was considered to be the best and highest-placed source the organisation had. So valued was he that he had his own dedicated FRU team of handlers in army headquarters, Lisbon. The complex they occupied was known within the organisation as the 'rat hole'.

Scap was so well known in Belfast that his pick-ups, drop offs, his cover stories and his alibis had to be suitably detailed and the rat-hole team was made up of exceptionally experienced and knowledgeable source handlers – the best in Northern Ireland at that time. Special Branch in the RUC were all too aware that Scap worked for the FRU and, on a few occasions, tried to take him out and replace him with one of their own sources. That was just how they rolled. Their consistently unhelpful attitude was a bit of a nuisance. They briefed one of their own sources within the IRA to badmouth Scappaticci to try and get him ousted from his position but he was far too savvy and his handlers were far too experienced to let that go through. Scap was, anyway, close with the people at the top of the tree within the terrorist organisation. It was just not going to happen.

Scap's cover was finally blown through newspaper articles and a book written by a vengeful ex-member of the FRU. Along with a co-author, he made the identity of the best informant in the IRA public. It was a bitter act as, while Scap had been involved with torture and murder, he had also passed information to the rat-hole detachment that saved many lives. He has probably prevented more deaths than any other human source in the province.

In 2016, Jon Boutcher, chief constable of Bedfordshire police, began Operation Kenova, an investigation into the alleged crimes carried out by Scappaticci. IRA members and personnel from the military and the intelligence services were quizzed about Scappaticci and their involvement with the man who was known within the intelligence community as 'Stakeknife'. Scappaticci has always denied being Stakeknife and said so in an interview broadcast from his solicitor's office. He then disappeared from Belfast. Boutcher's inquiry – ongoing at the time of writing – could have far-reaching and devastating outcomes for certain members of the intelligence community who would have known about Scappaticci's modus operandi and could therefore be found culpable as a result of his actions. I'm sure there is some twitching going on in certain Whitehall offices and I'm sure Boutcher's examination of the evidence will be roadblocked at many points. His inquiry submitted a number of files to the UK's director of public prosecutions, but proceedings against four people, two of them intelligence officers and one who actually worked for the prosecution service itself, have been thrown out. There are more files being reviewed by the Public Prosecution Service and it will be interesting to see if anyone will face charges for perjury, false imprisonment or assault. Of course, there are also murder inquiries as well. Yet I'll be very surprised if Jon Boutcher's team get any results: Whitehall is a very powerful and self-serving organisation.

When the stories about Stakeknife's true identity began to break, there was a huge amount of media interest. Everyone in the media wanted to be the one to track him down. I received a phone call from a one-time colleague, Jack, on behalf of the *News of the World*, who planned to doorstep Scappaticci over the allegations. I met the Irish editor, Alan, and his Northern Ireland editor, David, in a restaurant in Leeds and said I had never actually worked on the Stakeknife team personally, but I knew quite a bit about him. I had been an associate of the group of operators who made up his handlers and had a number of contacts in the police and military in the province. We had a pretty boozy afternoon in the city centre bistro and it was agreed that I should go to Northern Ireland, look up my old contacts and get every bit of information about Stakeknife's possible whereabouts. Believe it or not there had been rumours that he had been seen walking along the seafront eating an ice cream at Ballycastle, a small seaside town on the north coast of County Antrim. Personally, I felt it was more likely that he had been whisked away by the security services and was being debriefed and rebriefed about his cover stories and alibis. This would be a very trying time for Whitehall.

The chances were that Stakeknife would be in Kent, where the security services and the FRU had long maintained safe houses. These facilities were run by trained teams made up of those who had previously worked as handlers and known as resettlement – or 'R' – branch. They were geared up to run full and final debriefings in relative safety, put together packages for informants' future lives and ensure their anonymity.

Although the process usually ran quite smoothly there had been a few individuals who had suffered tragedies. One such case was that of Frank Hegarty who, like Stakeknife, had been an informant working for the FRU. It was rumoured that Hegarty returned to his beloved city of Derry after being assured of his safety by Martin McGuinness. Hegarty was subsequently kidnapped, tortured and murdered in 1986 by the Nutting Squad. The irony was that Stakeknife himself probably carried out the gruesome task, taking on a man who had played exactly the same role as himself for the intelligence services. At that point the IRA was falling apart from the inside out, thanks to informants in its ranks who were working for the police, army and the security services. The intelligence war was seemingly being won by the mainland British government although it would take more time and the political agreement before the Troubles were to de-escalate in any meaningful way. Unfortunately, all is not entirely calm even today and, at the time of writing – having spoken to a few of my contacts in recent years – it would appear that it is business as usual and the work to defeat terrorism continues much as it did back twenty or thirty years ago.

Despite my belief that the Home Counties were more likely locations in which to find Stakeknife, the newspaper people were keen that I go to Northern Ireland and within days I was landing in Belfast. I contacted an army mate who had since transferred into the RUC and we met up at the Europa hotel, a place I knew well from my former days in the FRU. It was well used by journalists in the Troubles and its high profile meant it was frequently bombed. We had a few beers over the course of the afternoon and chatted about previous jobs we had done together. He agreed that Stakeknife would have been got out of Northern Ireland a bit sharpish and, no, he did not have a clue where he was.

I called another mate who was quite knowledgeable about Belfast; he had worked in the city for years as a surveillance operative and had targeted Scappaticci on many occasions, although he had never been briefed about his role as a double agent for the British intelligence services. He knew the man's haunts well enough and he too had not seen him about for quite a while.

Just on the off chance that there was any truth to the Ballycastle rumour, I spent some days there. My options were quite limited: all I could really do was look around the place and visit pubs and hotels on the off-chance that Scappaticci might show up – which he didn't. I was not a bit surprised. My ex-surveillance mate in Belfast called to confirm that Scappaticci had vanished after his television appearance. His wife, however, had been seen in the area.

Back home, Jack said he would pass on the news, or lack of it, to the newspaper men. David himself later called with a humorous question: did I know a bloke called Rob Lewis who had written a book called *Fishers of Men* and, if I did, could I introduce them? Hilarious. I told him that I'd try.

Jack had called and asked me if I could do a matrimonial surveillance task for him on the outskirts of Harrogate in North Yorkshire. Some people would consider this type of job to be maybe a bit on the seedy side of life, but I always took them on. I was self-employed and earning pretty good money and getting all of my expenses and mileage covered so, why wouldn't I do them? They were invariably quite easy tasks as you would get snippets of information through from whoever the partner was who had asked for the surveillance to be carried out. That was always helpful. Matrimonial surveillance was always quite low risk as well, nothing like the surveillance operations I carried out in Northern Ireland which always had the chance of turning into a dangerous situation. However, on occasions being compromised was inevitable as there were long hours of being parked up in one spot for hours on end to try and get the evidence. The compromises were usually with neighbours and not usually the subject though.

I had taken two of the lads that I had done a number of jobs in London along with me, they were both good operators and had all the camera and video equipment needed to do this job.

We had been on this task for a few days when Nigel, one of the team rang me and asked if I could go to his location as he had a bit of a problem and could I call the other lad, Brian, to join us too. When I arrived with Nigel he was deep in conversation with two CID policemen in plain clothes, a local had called them to say that Nigel had been sat in his car just outside their house and they were very suspicious about him. The two coppers were a right old act and reminded me of the coppers in the TV series *Life on Mars*. Nigel had refused to tell them what he was doing there and they were giving him a seriously hard time.

When I turned up they immediately went into overdrive with me and actually said that if I did not tell them what I was doing there that they would take the three of us to the police station, take us into the cells and 'beat the fucking lives' out of us, they both kept saying 'We're North Yorkshire Police and we'll do what we fucking like'. All said in deep, typical North Yorkshire accents. It was hardly the crime of the century to be carrying out a matrimonial surveillance job and once I had disclosed what we were doing they calmed down. One of them took our driving licences back to their car and when he returned he asked, 'Which one of you fuckers is Lewis'. I told him that it was me and he waved his hand and gestured for me to follow him away from the others. He then announced that I was 'flagged' on their computer system and explained that all ex-servicemen who had training in firearms and escape and evasion methods were flagged in this way, he actually became quite friendly after that and asked about my past which he seemed genuinely interested in.

We packed away our kit and I drove home to await the next phone call.

SIX

I had been teamed up on a number of surveillance jobs with Bob Ruskin, an old-school East Ender from a civilian background. We got along like a house on fire; he was not only a great bloke but a good surveillance operative who was able to think on his feet.

Bob asked if I fancied doing a risky job, working alongside a black-cab driver and former member of the Met's flying squad. We were to pick up a woman from a refuge in Bedford and get her to the Old Bailey, where her solicitor would meet us in a special secure area. The youngster came from an Asian background and had been seeing a white British lad in defiance of her family. Her own father had ordered her brothers to kill her – a so-called 'honour killing', for having apparently brought shame on his family.

We carried out a few days' surveillance at the home of the father in Luton and identified and photographed the brothers who had been tasked with killing their sister. We were able to get our covert van close to the house and it proved to be easy to spot the male family members.

Bob and I picked up the subject from her safe house in Bedford and met Ian at Paddington station where she was transferred into his black cab. We drove through Marylebone on to Euston Square and on to Chancery Lane where we got her out of the cab and into the Old Bailey as quickly and as safely as we could. It had been decided at Paddington that I would go on ahead and wait at the entrance to the court to keep an eye out for either of the brothers and Bob would accompany the subject in Ian's cab. We kept in constant contact by mobile up to the last second. Throughout, Bob kept talking to the young woman, reassuring her that she was in safe hands. She was petrified.

Ian pulled the cab up directly outside the court and Bob and I got her straight inside with no problem at all. We met with her solicitor and the woman went off to one of the courtrooms to have her case heard. Bob and I had a wander around outside but saw nobody who might pose a threat when we got her out again. Nevertheless, Bob asked security guards if there was any alternative exit. They said they could let us out at the rear of the court, from where it was a short walk to Warwick Lane and Ian said he'd park up for the pickup. We decided this was a far better and safer option than retracing our steps.

We managed to get the girl out of the building, into the cab and I got back to my car without a hitch. At Paddington Ian showed us something that he had found under the rear bumper on his cab. It was a heavily cased, black plastic box with two very heavy-duty batteries, each double the size of a large mobile. Somebody had put a tracking device on his cab – but who? He was mystified. The police? Maybe a government department? Perhaps the black cab licensing authority?

Bob just grinned and held his hand out for the tracker, disappearing briefly. We next saw him with a massive smile on his face. 'They'll have some fun tracking that bastard.' Bob had gone to a platform and attached the device to a high-speed express to Swansea. We got back into my car and returned our charge to her refuge, safe and sound.

The following day Bob and I flew to Zurich, Switzerland, where Bob had been working for a manufacturing company on a long-term, on-and-off job. The CEO suspected one of his managers of selling information to a rival. Bob had carried out surveillance on a number of occasions but, so far, had found nothing untoward. The CEO offered us keys to the suspect manager's office but he didn't have any way of opening up the desk and filing cabinets. This would also have to be done without arousing the suspicions of the man under investigation and that would require a specialist. The only person I could think of was an Intelligence Corps mate who was qualified in what was known as 'method of entry' – or, to put it another way: lock-picking!

The owner agreed and we got my mate out the next day. By the evening, we were all at the factory, where the CEO opened up the manager's office and ushered in my man while we waited outside. When he came out after just thirty seconds my heart sunk. Our client glanced at him, but my mate just motioned casually to the office with his thumb and said, 'All done.' All the drawers and cabinets were open. The client laughed, saying that he wasn't sure whether my man was extremely good or his own office security was very useless. We hung around while the owner made his checks, before my mate locked everything up without damaging anything. We went to the hotel for a few beers and returned to London. We were never tasked by the factory owner again and so I assume that there was never any need for further tasking on this job, we almost certainly would have been called up to carry out any further enquiries he might want made.

A few days later I received another call from Bob. Did I fancy a trip to the seaside? I knew this was going to be interesting. It turned out we were going to Brixham, Devon, where I had attended my cousin's wedding the day I found out about the Chinook crash disaster. We were there now because scientific research laboratories and scientists' homes were being attacked, all with links to research involving animals who had attracted the attention of protest organisations. Our client was pharmaceutical company AstraZeneca, which had received advanced information from the police. Various laboratories of theirs were in danger of being hit by arson attacks. They needed to know how secure their locations were and our job was to see if it was possible to bypass security and get into their Brixham laboratory.

We sized up the facility for ourselves, at the site of a dead-end road in Freshwater Quarry, Brixham, next to a busy public car park that overlooked the harbour. There was no security fencing and no patrols; in fact, there was a side road to the right of the car park that anyone could use to reach the main door of the research building. There was one – very poorly maintained – barrier in the car park which was wide open. Security cameras were dotted around the main building, the laboratories and what looked like storage units to the rear.

We went back to our hotel to hatch a plan. We made mock incendiary devices out of half a dozen boxes of matches, electrical wire and small watch batteries. All we had to do now was get them into the building, note where we had left them and inform our client. Bob and I both carried letters of authority from the company that we would show should their security catch us or if we were to be picked up by police.

Getting in turned out to be far easier than we imagined it would be. That evening, after normal working hours, Bob strolled up to the main entrance and stood in a corner, a complete security blind-spot. The guard inside the foyer was anyway oblivious, reading a book instead of monitoring the CCTV screens. It was dark outside and the entrance hall was ablaze with light. We could see him clearly, but it was very difficult for him to spot us walking past outside. The plan was for me to act as a decoy. While Bob lurked in position, I rang the doorbell and the dozy security guard nearly jumped out of his skin. As he opened the swing doors I told him that someone at the far end of the building appeared to be trying to gain entry. He asked me to show him on the CCTV system and then I suggested we take a look outside and – incredibly – he agreed to abandon his post just like that and we wandered down the front of the building towards the car park. Bob nipped straight in before the doors shut. He knew he had a few minutes to complete the job while we were out and he jammed a plastic cone in place to hold the door open.

I slow-walked with the guard and ensured we took our time getting to the car park where, fortuitously, a vehicle unconnected to Bob and me was leaving at quite some speed. Perfect. I told the security guard that I thought that it was my suspect; even better, he was driving so quickly that the guard was unable to get any vehicle registration details. In reality, the vehicle was probably owned by no one more sinister than a boy racer practising his driving skills while there was nobody about. The guard continued checking the building with me in tow. We passed Bob, who simply strolled past us with a casual, 'Good evening, pleasant night.' I chatted on with the guard for another few minutes before making my excuses.

I got back to the hotel and Bob was already sat at the bar. He pointed at a pint of beer and said, 'There you go, son.' We contacted the head of security at AstraZeneca and Bob told him exactly where he could find our 'bombs'. Pleased with how the mission went, our client asked if we could go on to carry out a full security survey on the premises. We gave the place a really good going over and gave him a stack of recommendations to work on.

We left Brixham a day later and I've never been back.

Bob soon had another job; only this time I would be on my own. I was asked to take my camera with me and to go to the racecourse at Lingfield Park, Surrey. It was a pretty straightforward task – observe a specific race. When the winning horse was paraded I was to take photographs of everyone who went near to the animal and, in particular, anyone who touched or slapped it in congratulations. I had a pretty good HD camera that worked well at distance. Back home I would convert digital stills into .JPEG files. I was to email the images to Bob. That was it, no more information was forthcoming and I duly supplied half a dozen crisp images of the people who had contact with the winning horse. I naturally assumed that it was connected with doping but some clients do not give you the full story as to why they want tasks doing and it would have been out of order for me to ask anything further.

I missed out on a trip to Havana because I was involved in carrying out surveillance for another routine insurance claim. I was tied to it for a week or so and the client was one of my best, Allianz Cornhill. It was while I was working that my friend Mike dangled the prospect of well-paid work for a couple of months in Cuba, but I had to sign up to his team in the next couple of days. I would have loved to have gone, but I wasn't prepared to break my commitment and regretfully I declined. I would later be very glad about my decision, and not just because I had honoured my agreement.

I heard that Mike's team deployed to Havana on the understanding that they were carrying out a matrimonial investigation on behalf of a firm of solicitors working for a wealthy Cuban lady. Was the commission all it seemed? Many of us in the surveillance industry have long suspected that some high-risk jobs are in reality ordered by security services creating a personal cover story in case the team are compromised. This was what happened in this case. The team were arrested at their hotel and detained in a grim jail for forty-eight days, subsisting on a meagre diet. The girlfriend of one of the men had flown out to take a few days' holiday and, unfortunately for her, she also was imprisoned. After tangled political and consular problems were eventually solved, they were allowed home. Rumour had it that the release was personally authorised by Fidel Castro himself.

In my work for Allianz Cornhill I would come across some quite unusual behaviour. Fraudulent claimants would go to quite unbelievable lengths to back up their stories and win massive payouts from the industry. I had to assemble evidence to reduce or even invalidate claims entirely. One particularly outrageous claimant had stolen a car and filled it with petrol from a garage in Milton Keynes without paying. The police identified the vehicle and set off in a pursuit that reached speeds of over a hundred miles an hour, at which point the driver lost control, hurtling off the road and rolling down an embankment. The driver, taken to hospital, was arrested. So far, so sadly all too common. But then the car thief came up with the bright idea of claiming against the owner of the vehicle he had stolen. He said the car was poorly maintained as he – the thief – was an excellent driver and would never have crashed. There must, he believed, have been something wrong with the car. The insurance company had to pay out for an independent inspection and proved the vehicle was in top roadworthy condition. The car thief had his claim thrown out of court.

I had put a lot of time and effort into both of these surveillance tasks and had gathered a lot of video footage that had shown that they were both just leading normal lives and their injury claims were both very suspect.

Another criminal trying his luck came from Stoke-on-Trent, where he had been in the process of carrying out a burglary on a supermarket when he fell through a skylight and injured himself quite badly. He said that he would have been OK if the building had been properly maintained and checked; another instance of pure, brass-necked audacity. Luckily, I was able to get a load of evidence on the lifestyle of this character and his claim against Allianz Cornhill was dismissed.

When I was not doing surveillance, close protection or carrying out other investigations I would often serve legal documents on behalf of solicitors and companies. The usual method of serving papers on people was quite straightforward and after they had accepted the documents I then had to go to a solicitors office and swear an affidavit on oath to say that I had carried out the task. The solicitor would normally charge a few pounds in cash for this as it only ever took about five minutes to complete. There was one individual who was illegally printing and distributing pornographic magazines from a lock-up in Dartford, London. He ripped off the name and design of a respectable publication, having changed one letter in the title. An extremely slippery character, this fellow had evaded several attempts to serve him with a cease-and-desist order. Whether the papers were delivered or not, he simply denied he'd seen them.

I knew it would be best to nab him just at the moment as he was walking up the steps that led to his terraced property. My first move was to park my car over the road, setting up my trusty covert camera. I knew roughly what time to expect him and made sure I wasn't too close to the car or the house. I had about two hours of recording time; plenty. I hid myself at a point near enough to have his front door in view. I approached to meet him as he arrived and called his name just as he opened his front door.

'Yes? What do you want?' Got him! I served the papers and made a note of the time. As I walked down his steps the entire bundle of legal papers hit me on the back of my head with some force. Not my problem – he had been served and it was all on film. I was sure to leave the pile of scattered paperwork where it lay and ambled away from the house and my car, only returning an hour or so later. He had no idea that a camera had been filming him from the vehicle. I reviewed the video footage at home. The next day I swore an affidavit at the solicitor's office. The client was said to have been well pleased with the result and the pornographer was closed down, his printing equipment removed by court bailiffs.

These cases could be complicated. I had once to check a property for a silver Mercedes that had been taken by a man to settle a debt. I had court papers that allowed me to visit what was the site of a Gypsy encampment. As part of my job, I was permitted to seek police backup in cases where there might be a threat of violence and on this occasion I did go to the police station in Dunstable, who called out to a patrol car to support me. Within a few minutes of the request being made, a police inspector wearing what was pretty much full riot gear turned up and I was escorted to the site with two riot vans and eight officers. The police, they said, were always careful to come out to the site in numbers but more positively, I had chosen the right time because most of the residents would still be in bed with hangovers. It was a dramatic job but the car in question was gone – probably, the police suggested, already resprayed and moved.

It was not the only job that didn't end in success. Allianz Cornhill had me working once on a sensitive inquiry. A woman from Paris had been visiting her sister in London with her son. While in the UK, the child was sadly run over by a lorry and had to be cut out by the fire service. He had been jammed into a front wheel arch and suffered quite drastic injuries. After he was eventually released from hospital, the two returned to Paris and made a claim against the lorry company via a firm of French solicitors. I was sent to Paris to observe the mother and child, who lived on a tough estate that had seen many anti-racist riots and where the residents were wary of strangers. I spent three days trying to do surveillance when, unbelievably, not one person came out or went in that block of flats. It was frustrating and strange. I went back a month later with exactly the same result – not a single person, never mind the claimant, came out of the building. The job stalled.

Around this time, Bob invested heavily in electronic equipment for locating listening devices and bugs. He had been tasked with sweeping boardrooms and private houses and cars. Bob knew that I was good with computers and especially skilled at detecting malware, software maliciously installed on a device to report back to another party. Together, Bob and I were able to offer his clients a full and thorough service, reassuring them that they were not being bugged or monitored either physically or via cyber methods. It was quite a lucrative little number.

Ahead of a mergers and acquisitions meeting at a financial organisation on the Edgware Road, London, we were asked to check if the boardroom was under surveillance. Bob's electronic equipment was fired up and we were soon scanning and monitoring a number of frequencies. Bingo! A hostile signal was detected; there was undoubtedly some kind of device in the room and all we had to do now was find out where it was. This was the old-fashioned bit. It was all very well using technological wizardry to tell us that somebody was up to no good but when it came to finding out where they were hiding, nothing beat good old 'Eyeballs Mk 1.0'. We eventually discovered the intruder – a small circular device, no bigger than a two-pence piece – attached to the back of a standard lamp. We reported back to the managing director – in a different part of the office.

He was impressed and decided that he wanted it left in place. His plan was to go ahead with the meeting, re-writing his notes and misdirecting the briefing in an exercise in disinformation. Quite a clever ploy. The board of the company were all given advance notice. In the meantime, he asked us to continue searching and monitoring and he was particularly keen that we electronically sweep his own office. Sure enough, we found a further two devices that were live and active – one in his own office and one in the office used by the financial director. The MD was absolutely livid that someone had been able to gain access and plant these bugs. As his was a high-value organisation with plenty of competitors, he knew their activities might have been monitored over a length of time.

The board meeting went ahead and he duly threw in a number of fake statements. Bob and I went back about two weeks later, ran the detecting equipment again and this time removed the bugs, which ended up in the River Thames. The MD asked us to go to his home that weekend – a very plush mansion in the Hampstead Heath area – where nothing was detected. We continued with fortnightly Sunday afternoon visits to his office for some six months and nothing further was found, but it was a very useful source of income for us that year.

SEVEN

The close protection (bodyguarding) market in this country is dominated by retired SAS men. Any gaps are filled by those who have come from specialist backgrounds such as 14 INT and FRU. I was lucky enough to be involved in several decent close-protection jobs over the years, sometimes working directly with the principal (the focus of the task) or supporting the main team.

Support was my role at one magnificent property in the Regent's Park. The Holme is an imposing Georgian mansion in the centre of the park, owned by the Saudi royal family. This is where high-ranking Saudis and diplomats come to stay in London. I was working with three retired ex-presidential bodyguards from the CIA. They looked after the principal, a Saudi diplomat, while a team of eight ex-SAS and 14 INT blokes made up the foot soldiers working the grounds and gates. I was invited to join by the team leader, an old friend. Although my job only involved wandering the gardens at night and checking general security, it was very well paid.

I moved straight on to a similar role with another Saudi, a self-made businessman who was extremely wealthy. This particular sheikh was a bit of a rogue. He was staying in the luxurious presidential suite on the top floor of the Hilton on Park Lane, London. He had an entourage of mainly Lebanese men and told me that Saudis like the way the Lebanese talk. I was not sure how true his statement was more generally, but it worked for him. They would bring bags of khat, a stimulant that induces euphoria – and is now banned in the UK. The sheikh wandered around the hotel with a wad of fifty-pound notes that he would hand out to any member of staff who said 'Hello' to him, as well as those manning the reception desk. The doormen and concierge staff were all given handouts as well.

Strangely, when the sheikh went out of the hotel it was without any of his close protection staff. Our role was to hang out in the suite and we spent most of our time just sat around in the kitchen area. The sheikh and his many Lebanese pals had a great passion for Johnnie Walker whisky and call girls. There was a constant procession of scantily dressed blonde girls at any one time and the sheikh would take two or three of them into his room at regular intervals. When they were told they could go, they were all handed a thousand pounds in fifty-pound notes by the sheikh's manager.

The sheikh had at length to fly back to Jeddah for Ramadan, leaving under the strict instructions of his elder brother. He confided that he would have preferred spending the month in Rio de Janeiro.

It was back to the Hilton for another Saudi family, allegedly including a prince and princess. They took over two entire floors of the prestigious address with the top level reserved for the prince and his entourage. My contact for this job was their business manager, a Polish guy called Tomasz. He was a nice enough bloke working out of Knightsbridge, London, and was responsible for their accommodation, vehicles and flights whenever they came to the UK. My team included Gary and Liz, who was ex-military police. Our main principal was the princess and we had a remit to transfer to the prince when he went out, including the day he made an abortive trip to the Ritz. The prince fancied their afternoon tea but while he was ready to go in baggy shorts and shirts with sandals, Gary and I wore smart suits and ties. We got no further than the foyer of the hotel, where the prince was asked where he thought he was going. He indignantly declared that he had a reservation but the firm response was, 'Your friends can come in,' meaning us, his security detail, 'but you cannot while you are so attired.' The prince stormed out, absolutely fuming and we had to turn tail and follow him home to the Hilton.

The princess had more success when she went to Regent's Park to meet her mother and sister in one of the cafés. Gary sat on the table next to the party while I went to pick up their coffees. The princess tried to pay me for the round with a thousand pounds in cash. I took one of the fifty-pound notes from the wodge and handed back the rest, explaining that was enough to cover the cost of the coffees for her entire trip. She gave me a strange look and told me to keep the lot. So, day two of the job and me and Gary were already up five hundred quid each; result. She was very generous with her gifts. When she went to Savile Row, Mayfair, world-famous for gentleman's outfitters and tailors, she told me to pick some items for myself. Again, I turned her offer down at first, but she was pretty insistent and I picked two silk ties of regiments in which I had served and a set of hand-engraved blazer buttons with my regimental crest. All very nice too, and very expensive.

The princess had a division made up of Filipino women; they attended to her every whim and were always rushing around the place doing her bidding. Almost all had children. Apparently, the team had looked after her mother all through her pregnancy and had been encouraged to have children at the same time as the princess was born; the offspring all played together around us as well. Her closest maid did not like us at all and was always having a dig for standing too close to the princess.

One evening, Gary and I took her to her sister's place in Bayswater. We were to stay outside until she was ready to be taken back to the Hilton. For a few hours we could hear shrieks of laughter coming from inside; they were partying hard. Through the net curtains we could see the princess, her sister and some other women dancing around and drinking. There was a lot of drinking. She eventually left at about five o'clock in the morning, totally off her head, and we had to manhandle her into the back of the Mercedes to get her home. I phoned ahead to the duty security manager at the hotel, a good bloke I'd known for years. He agreed to open the tradesman's entrance at the side of the building. We were able to drive in and use the service lift to get our charge up to her floor without letting her be seen by any member of the public or even by the foyer staff.

Gary and I propped her up in the lift until we could help her out when we reached her corridor. The Filipino women and their kids were still up and about, cleaning, sorting and generally reorganising the princess's clothes and belongings from one room to another; she must have had some thirty suitcases. The member of her staff who had already taken against us was now absolutely furious at the sight of Gary and I daring to touch her charge, much less haul the paralytic princess around the hotel. She wasn't much happier that we'd bought Her Highness up in the service lift.

I bluntly said that we could not possibly have brought royalty through the public main door in the state she was in; what if she had been seen? The top maid did back off a bit at that and I left her to carry the princess to her room.

The following evening the princess asked me for a favour. She was very big friends with Sana bin Laden, the stepsister of the infamous Osama bin Laden. It was Sana's birthday and she wanted me to arrange for a massive floral arrangement of a thousand red roses to be delivered to her apartment in Lowndes Square, Belgravia. It was already 10 p.m. and she wanted it this same day. Even the reliable reception concierge was stumped at this one. He agreed to contact the florist with the shop in the lower ground floor of the hotel and pass on my number. Fortunately, she rang just five minutes later and I told her my predicament. She was able to come to my rescue; she had roses in the shop and knew a supplier who could deliver the rest. I was amazed and told her to charge what she liked – think of an obscene amount, I suggested, and then double it. Gary and I managed to deliver the resulting huge display down to Lowndes Square before the day was out.

When the princess wanted to go to visit the antiques shops at the end of the King's Road, Chelsea, she was on the hunt for ornate, gold-framed mirrors to export to her home in Saudi Arabia. While she never once inquired as to the prices, the mirrors I saw were astronomically expensive. She still had to make her final decision and returned to the hotel. I took the opportunity to nip back and asked each shop owner if I could have a percentage of the asking price if I ensured that the princess came to their premises? Each owner agreed, writing a figure on the back of their business cards. They didn't seem put out by my request and I guessed this was a frequent occurrence. To my very good fortune, the princess ended up ordering many items from all of the shops we had visited. When she finally departed the UK I was able to collect a significant amount in commission; it was a good day.

I also accompanied the princess when she wanted to get her hair and nails done. Nicky Clarke was the renowned stylist of the day with his salon in Carlos Place, Mayfair, pulling in a large celebrity clientele. If you were an A-lister, it was where you had to have your hair done. It was indeed a very classy place and, after Clarke was finished, it was over to a little Chinese lady to get nails varnished and polished. The beautician asked if the princess also wanted her fortune told, but she didn't – suggesting I might like a go. While doing the princess's nails the manicurist asked me some general questions about my life and, astoundingly, guessed my birthday. She needed to know the day of my birth and, interested to see where this was going, I phoned my mum and it turned out I was born at around eight o'clock on a Monday morning. After I told my mother I'd explain later, the nail technician then proceeded to reel off a load of facts about my family that were all spot on, including the fact that I had 'worn a uniform for a number of years' and that it was mostly coloured green. So accurate was this that I wondered if it was a joke and that maybe the princess had fed her some information she had got from Gary, who knew me and my family well, and was waiting for us out in the car. No such thing; it was all totally genuine. Quite amazing.

On the day the job eventually came to a close, we all lined up outside the Hilton, a row of black Mercedes cars for the family and minibuses for the Filipino workforce and their kids. At Heathrow we were allowed to drive through the airside entrance – straight on to the tarmac and up to the stairs of their 747 plane. No passport control for the Saudi royalty and Tomasz told me the airliner was just one of a fleet of three they owned. The princess boarded the plane without so much as a thank-you or farewell although, when Tomasz handed me a brown envelope and said, 'A gift from the princess,' I did see it contained a thousand pounds in fifty-pound notes. That was more than a thank-you.

The film world was to make a change from the Saudi elite, with a movie job coming via a call from a contact I knew well. Following allegations that Hollywood star Mel Gibson had made homophobic remarks, threats had been made against both him and his family. The man himself was now in Scotland, filming what would be his William Wallace epic, *Braveheart*, and my task would be to assess security and make suggestions; all pretty straightforward. I was a bit taken back, however, when I learned I had to immediately drive to Fort William, Scotland, for a breakfast meeting the very next day with a location manager from the production company. I was told I had to meet him at the Alexandra hotel and packed my bags to start the seven-hour journey northwards.

The Alexandra itself was booked out but I managed to secure at least my first night's accommodation at the nearby West End hotel. Liam Neeson was in the area filming *Rob Roy* and every hotel and guest house in the area were absolutely rammed with cast, crew and production teams. I was lucky to get anything at that point. My destination in the morning was not too far away and I found Mel Gibson to be a really good bloke. We chatted easily, he seemed very interested about my background and we got along very well. He was not too concerned about the threats, remarking that he had had them all his life. It was the production company which had taken them very seriously.

I went to inspect the house in which Gibson and his family were staying, a typical, large country property. For me there was one immediate problem – it was situated on a main road; anyone could drive straight in and be outside the house. I suggested we find a more remote and secure property to rent and visited a few estate agents with the location manager to find the perfect place. Our selection was remote and, best yet, had security fencing, electronic gates and movement-sensing lighting. When its alarm system was triggered, the alert was monitored by a security company. It ticked all the boxes and, importantly, Gibson liked his new digs. There was good news on the accommodation front for me too, as a regular guest at the West End had cancelled, leaving the room free for me for the duration of the gig.

What I had not bargained for, though, was the reaction of Robyn Gibson, the star's wife, to the move: she was fuming. This was tricky, as the idea was that I would be working with her, as Gibson already had a personal bodyguard and driver. My role was supposed to be to ensure the safety and security of the family, but when I spoke to her at the house it was pretty obvious she had taken an instant dislike and was not keen for me to play any role for her and their six kids. I asked if she'd prefer me to be out with them, as part of the family, or discreetly shadowing. She told me to return to my hotel and that she would call if she wanted me, 'which will not be anytime soon'. It was the first and last time we spoke.

I reported back to my bosses, who said I should just stay in the area and be available. I thought it prudent to introduce myself at the local police station. The local police inspector, a really good bloke by the name of Colin Blake, was very supportive and told me that I could call him any time. We met again that night, when I ran into him in the hotel bar, next door to his office. I discovered that he lived almost two hours away in Inverness and travelled down on Sundays for his week's work.

I spent my days driving around the local area, visiting the film sets and doing the occasional drive past to check the house. I felt I needed to do something even if it was not wanted. When I got a chance to speak to Gibson he just shrugged and told me to make a holiday of my stay. I spent most evenings in the bar at the hotel chatting to Colin and a leader of the Lochaber district mountain rescue team named Willie.

One night Colin suggested a beer at the local golf club. He phoned what he said was a taxi and ten minutes later a police officer walked in. 'Your taxi is outside, sir,' she said. I couldn't quite believe that our cabbie for the night would be an official police car.

'I'm the local sheriff, Rob,' Colin explained, 'so that is my taxi.'

There were some differences with a regular cabbie, as I discovered when we came across a car driving the wrong way around a roundabout. 'I really can't ignore that, sir,' said the uniformed driver, looking at Colin in the rear-view mirror. Colin agreed, we spun around and headed after the errant vehicle, sirens blazing and blue lights flashing. The miscreant was a Dutch tourist who apologised profusely for what he promised was only a lapse in concentration. He was given a talking-to and sent on his way. Fort William, the base for those who want to tackle Ben Nevis, attracts large number of tourists and Colin said that the police generally tended to advise foreign drivers rather than be any more heavy-handed.

I went with Colin and Willie when they accompanied the procurator fiscal (the Scottish version of a public prosecutor) up Ben Nevis, to assist in his investigation of the claims of a woman who said her husband had slipped on the mountain and fallen, out of sight, into one of the many crags. When we reached the point given as the site of the accident, Colin and Willie were instantly dismissive of the tale. Firstly, they would have expected body parts strewn over the rocks and, secondly, Willie had himself been involved in a rescue in that area two days earlier and was certain there was no body. We headed back to Fort William.

This would be my last evening in the town. It was obvious that my job was a non-starter and, having ensured that the Gibson family were now staying in a safer and more secure location, it was time to move on. My next role was going to be waiting for me back in London and it was assigned by the same person who had introduced me to the *Braveheart* company. Hopefully, I thought, it would prove less frustrating. I wandered through the town one last time with Colin. He was greeted by everyone young and old, knew all of them by name and inquired about members of their families as well. I was quite impressed. I asked if there was any chance of getting hold of a salmon to take home and he promised to introduce me to the daughter of a well-known local poacher. To my great surprise, she turned out to be the police officer from the previous evening and she dropped off a salmon at the hotel the next morning. I headed south accompanied by an eight-pound fresh fish, wrapped in newspaper and packed with ice.

My new charges were also Hollywood elite, Tom Cruise and Nicole Kidman. He was shooting *Mission: Impossible* (1997) and she was working on *Portrait of a Lady* (1996). The couple were staying in a Holland Park mansion, where neighbours included Richard Branson and Simon Cowell. They had been getting a lot of press attention and the paparazzi were getting to be a right nuisance, targeting their two children. The nannies were being physically hassled, with camera lenses forced in the children's faces. Photographers stood on makeshift ladders in the road, trying to catch them as a family in the house and in the garden. Police helped to disperse the paparazzi, up to a point, but they would just return later.

On more than one occasion I also had to ask the photographers to back off and respect the family's privacy, but I managed to establish a fairly decent rapport with most of them. On one occasion I was in the park with Kidman for her eldest child's nursery school sports day. I didn't know how the paparazzi managed it but within a few minutes there were loads of them. I asked politely that they keep their distance; there was no need to get so close. They all had massive lenses and they knew very well they could have stood a hundred metres away and got pretty decent shots. One of the snappers called out my name and I picked out an old army mate among the throng, stood there with a couple of cameras with the obligatory huge lenses hanging around his neck.

He had left the services a few years before and had been doing this ever since. He asked if I could tip him off when both Cruise and Kidman were both with the children: nobody had managed to get that particular photograph. It would sell well, he said, and he would bung me a decent amount. I replied, 'Nice try, mate, but I'd never get another day's work if I did that.' He shrugged his shoulders and laughed.

Next door to the house used by Cruise and Kidman, I had noticed two blokes on a number of occasions. They wore suits and ties and could be seen wandering around or stood at the back door watching the garden. It turned out they were both from the Met's diplomatic protection unit and were looking after a visiting foreign dignitary. Both were pretty obviously armed, judging by the bulges on their right hips and both had been members of the Royal Military Police, where they had fulfilled a similar role.

Cruise once asked me if I wanted to go to the studios with him; he was a really nice bloke and, in a typically American way, he was very courteous as well. He sat in the front with his driver and I was in the back when we came across a car broken down on the Hogarth roundabout. It was causing major problems for the traffic and its young lady driver was obviously flustered. Cruise told his driver to pull over and he and I helped the woman push her car off the road to a safe place. She kept glancing at Tom, then looking at me in a quizzical way and looking back at the star. I nodded, 'Yes – he is.' Her face was a picture and I wondered how many of her family and friends would believe her when she told them that Tom Cruise had come to her rescue on the road.

Cruise was friends with Dustin Hoffman, who was also in London at the same time with his son and they would all play with a basketball in Hyde Park. I had to shoo away the paparazzi one day, but they were good about moving on – probably heard that Princess Diana had been spotted in a restaurant nearby or something.

I worked with the couple for a good while and really enjoyed it. Even though they were pretty much Hollywood royalty they were both really nice people and I got along fine with both of them.

EIGHT

I had been working for various security and investigation companies in London for a number of years, mainly in Mayfair. I had got to know a number of people who socialised after office hours in the area and had found the pubs and restaurants full of individuals who could be quite interesting. I had a good number of contacts, some of whom became close friends.

One of these was Andrew Cameron, who had been in newspaper publishing for years before taking over *Penthouse* UK as CEO, a franchise of the soft-porn empire of American Bob Guccione. Cameron employed two other friends, Nikki and her partner Simon, who also became good friends. They began to work on the re-launch of the magazine and promoting the *Penthouse* brand. One of their ideas to publicise the publication took the form of a party in a posh Mayfair hotel with a load of *Penthouse* 'Pets', as the models were called, working as waitresses. Bob Guccione and his daughter, Nina, would be in attendance. The other key idea was forming a *Penthouse* Pets dance troupe to tour various nightclubs throughout the country.

I was to provide two close protection bodyguards for Guccione and transport the dance troupe around the UK, for which I was put on an attractive monthly retainer. The Gucciones were to stay at the hotel I knew so well, the Hilton, Park Lane, where I had personal contact with the security. I recruited two ex-SAS guys to act as security throughout the trip, Mike and John. They were very capable and I knew I could entrust them to do the job professionally. The party went really well and was awash with drinks and snacks.

The dance troupe, meanwhile, set to work with a choreographer outside Heathrow and at the end of each day I ferried them all home; they did work hard, fair play to them and eventually worked up a pretty good show. Nikki and Simon booked up the tour and once we hit the road we were soon in a routine in which I would liaise with security prior to the girls taking to the stage. We toured half a dozen nightclubs and the only troublesome evening was one when we paid a visit to a club in Wrexham where some lads in the audience got a bit out of hand. The bouncers sorted them out while I got the girls safely out of the back door and away in the minibus.

You would think that looking after a troupe of attractive dancers would be a great job to have as a bloke: however, in reality, it was a complete pain in the neck. The girls were extremely petulant and argumentative; they would always want to stay on at the clubs long after their show to go on drinking and dancing. Even after the fiasco at Wrexham one of them said that she wanted to stay and that she would find her own way back home. I simply had to insist that she got in the minibus and, eventually, she did.

The first edition of the relaunched magazine ran with a James Bond theme, featuring all the cars, the weapons and pieces of equipment used in the movies. A Pierce Brosnan lookalike was hired for the photoshoot alongside glamorous girls. I provided security with Mike in the old warehouse that had been rented for the day. Nikki arrived with two models who, I have to say, were quite plain and not at all glamorous. However, when I saw their shoot in the magazine itself, they looked stunning. It's amazing to see what a bit of lighting and make-up and Photoshop can do. At the end of the day, Mike and I decided to head into Mayfair for a few beers.

Mike had written *CQB: Close Quarter Battle*, that detailed his time in the Falkland Islands with the Parachute Regiment and in the SAS. He had also been the firearms and self-defence instructor at the training headquarters of the FRU. Mike asked if I had ever thought about publishing something on my time in the army. Our discussion planted a seed in my mind: I had a couple of weeks' holiday due and was not going away anywhere. I decided to start writing my memoirs. Armed with a load of photographs and memories I found it relatively easy to write about my work.

I asked an old friend who worked as a newspaper editor if he'd mind giving me feedback. He was very complimentary and was really interested about my previous life.

Enthused, I went back to work while fielding inquiries from various people about how it was progressing. My friends and acquaintances weren't the only ones expressing an interest. The Ministry of Defence soon wrote to warn me that I would need to let them vet the contents ahead of any publishing deal. Who alerted the MoD? I had a good idea – one of my Mayfair crowd who I reckoned had a bit of a jealous streak. I never got him to admit it.

I emailed the manuscript to the government's D notice committee in Whitehall, the board responsible for vetting sensitive information. They invited me to a meeting at the MoD to which I was instructed to attend on my own. It was an austere event – I was offered a hard, plastic office chair on one side of the table, where I faced three similar chairs. The middle chair was occupied by a man in a pinstriped suit and some sort of school or university tie. The other two interviewers included a former commissioned member of my old unit who was now at the MoD. Aside from an ordnance survey map of Northern Ireland on the wall behind them, the room was bare – no pictures, paintings, furniture; nothing. A copy of my manuscript was on the desk in front of the man in the middle and he was the first to speak. If I decided to continue publication, he warned, I was likely to face a prison sentence. I stood up to bring the meeting to a close. Talk of prison meant I needed legal representation. They asked me to hear them out.

The interviewer continued, they were not stopping me from getting my book published at all. Some content was, in his opinion, in breach of national security and would need to be thoroughly vetted before I could take it to a publishing company. That same line about national security was repeated time and again.

At length, we agreed that the MoD would go over the manuscript and indicate deletions by scoring through lines with a marker pen. It seemed straightforward enough, but they kept the book for about three months and I badgered them on a weekly basis until eventually they returned my work, completely annihilated. It made me think their plan had been to redact so much that I would give up on the project. Whatever the real motivation, I was determined to get it done. I spent months visiting the MoD on a fortnightly basis. I would sit and be informed that certain chapters had to be removed completely and those that remained would have to have massive portions rewritten.

Some of the instructions were just barmy. I was told to take out the name of the camp that housed our detachment because it would endanger present-day operations. Didn't they know it had been demolished years earlier? I asked. They didn't. Was I sure? they asked. I said the site was now a runway at Enniskillen airport. The interviewer excused himself, returning after about ten minutes (presumably of swift, last-minute checking), coughed heavily and said, 'Right, ahem, let's move on.' This was farcical: the Northern Ireland section of the MoD were not aware of major changes to their own field of operations. It was the same with his next point, that a description of a woman was too close to reality and had to be excised – except that it wasn't and anyway she had died. Cue another abrupt break for a fact-check.

And so it went on. I did rewrite after rewrite but remained determined to get the all-clear. I understood the reasoning for the vetting and had no objection to it being overseen by the D notice committee but, when we got down to it, their comments often seemed totally irrelevant and often petty. I was told that I might even have to change the title of the book as the MoD could claim 'Fishers of Men' was the motto of their Force Research Unit. The phrase was originally taken from the Gospel of Matthew, I observed, and if the MoD claimed copyright over the Bible, we were all in trouble.

Further discussions were held over the use of photographs. We agreed that I would black out or pixelate faces. No photographs of St Angelo should be used, even though we had ascertained that the camp did not exist anymore (I did use two pictures taken inside the facility, with just a brick wall as background visible).

My contact at the committee even asked me to insert a few lines on their behalf, in order to correct a scenario that had been wrongly described in someone else's book, which I thought was quite a funny request. With that, we were almost there – or so I thought. The following week I was told that I could get the book published, having by then lost over two hundred pages and had to change some of my storylines. Not so fast – I was then called back once more to the MoD to find the goalposts had been moved again. Now I was told that I had to sign various non-disclosure documents. The MoD had brought along their own legal advisor and I complained that I had should have been allowed to call on a solicitor too. I was told I could do that retrospectively – get advice on the NDA after the meeting and only after I'd signed it. What use was that? I said I'd have to call my solicitor first, who agreed to me signing the confidentiality agreement for the meeting but nothing else. It was rapidly descending into farce. The MoD representative said that was not good enough and we left it there. It was quite a long old haul, but *Fishers of Men* was finally published in late 1999.

I was still in contact with Andrew Cameron at *Penthouse*, who introduced me to his friend Nick, the owner of three London hostess bars. Westminster council employees were working undercover in the venues as part of their role in issuing club licences, monitoring full-time staff along with sub-contractors, including the girls themselves. Nick was concerned that the girls could be encouraged to arrange after-hours meetings with men who hinted in the club that they could pay them for sex. This would be a breach of the licencing regulations. The hostesses had all been very well-briefed about these possible approaches and how to handle them, but Nick needed to find out if any of the girls were likely to be open to such an approach. He also wanted to look into the bar staff of the clubs, as takings had dropped quite a bit in recent months and he didn't know if that was due to a lack of customers or if someone was dipping their fingers in the till. It was not dramatic, he said, but the nightly cashing-up had become a bit lighter than he had predicted.

The establishments' clientele were largely middle-aged blokes, quite well-off, who would generally pay by cash. Hostesses encouraged them to buy champagne and they would then chat and drink with their male customers. The girls perfected the art of emptying their glasses surreptitiously while hardly drinking anything. The men were coaxed into buying more champagne and enjoying further company, and discouraged from leaving their tables and becoming distracted, thanks to table service. A barman would take the order, return to the table with the drinks, the blokes would hand over cash and the barman would bring change and a receipt. It was rare that a punter would actually check the receipt and, invariably, the leftover cash was left as a tip.

I suggested that I test the system by taking up a table and feeding in notes marked with a unique scribble; the clubs were dark and nobody would notice. I would remember which barman served me and, when Nick and his wife cashed up at the end of the night, they could check which – if any – marked notes had failed to make it to the till. Over the course of a number of weeks I became a regular visitor to the clubs, where I would drop in marked notes and make subtle hints to each hostess that there could be 'extra earnings' for meeting out of hours. I ran this line with a dozen girls and, fair play to them, not a single one took the bait. They all either steered our conversation in a different direction or flat-out said that they were not allowed to meet clients outside of their employment. Nick felt a lot happier when he heard the news.

The same could not be said of the bar staff. I had fifty-pound notes from Nick to spend in the clubs, each of which he had marked. I used them to pay for champagne and the following day I would let him know who had served me and how many fifty-pound notes I had passed over. It was soon obvious that not all the notes were returning to Nick at two of his venues. We monitored the pattern of missing money over a few weeks to be sure and then he sacked both barmen involved.

Nick and Andrew invited me to Ascot and we had a great time, although Cameron had bad news to share about *Penthouse*. Apparently, the sales of the relaunch were terrible and Andrew was throwing the towel in before his finances were completely drowned. This also meant that Nikki and Simon were to leave as well and, from my personal perspective, my retainer would end with the *Penthouse* tours. It was bad news for all concerned, really.

I continued to socialise in the Shepherd Market area of Mayfair, where I had got to know Andrew; it was still a great place for making contacts. We used to use a private club that was run by an ex-SAS bloke; it was in a small side street and was entered by a rather innocuous door that most people would not even notice. Once through the door you then went up a flight of stairs and entered the bar that was used by a number of well-known retired footballers. Most evenings you would find the likes of George Best, Denis Law and Eddie Gray at the bar, I got to know Best quite well and sometimes we would leave the club and go to Dover Street wine bar, a favourite hangout for shady characters. The two brothers who ran the place were like an Italian version of the Kray twins. I always got the feeling they were seriously dodgy: luckily, they liked me and I got on well with them.

My brother got to meet George Best one day, when he popped up to meet me in Mayfair for a few beers. In his younger days, my brother had been a massive Manchester United fan and had idolised the likes of George and Denis. Back then he had posters up of all the stars on his bedroom walls. We had a couple of drinks in the Irish pub and then wandered to the bar around the corner where we met George and I introduced them. The night before I had been in the Dover Street with George and his wife Angie when he ran out of cash and I subbed him. Imagine the look on my brother's face when the legendary George Best gave me a twenty-pound note and thanked me for the loan. We were joined by Pat 'Paddy' Crerand, another massive name at Celtic and Manchester United back in the sixties. My brother was in legend heaven. He still talks about it to this day.

NINE

A mate had entered into a joint venture with a recruitment company in Manchester and made a lot of money when he eventually sold up to a venture capital firm.

The MD of the outfit that bought him out, Mark, happened to mention that he had a suspicion one of his managers was up to something. She supplied temporary staff to offices throughout the area and her profit margins had sunk and the number of clients had diminished. My mate thought of me as an investigator and introduced the MD, who was interested in me taking a look at her to see if I could glean any information.

I drove around the area and walked near her office and house just to get a general feel for the scene. She lived in a very exclusive part of Milton Keynes, in a large detached property with a decent driveway and land. There was a brand-new Audi outside the front door. The office was also in the fashionable part of what was referred to as MK1. She was obviously doing extremely well and had been on the verge of being invited to be a board director at the parent company in Manchester when things started going downhill.

The next morning, I plotted up just down the road from her house and started surveillance, intending to build up a picture of her daily routine. She left the house in another car, a black, very smart, brand-new BMW, and headed towards the area of central

Milton Keynes. It was pretty easy to follow as there were a lot of other cars heading into the area. She parked up in a designated space, went to fetch items from the boot of the car and then walked with her briefcase into an office complex; her office was on the top floor of the three-storeyed building. I managed to photograph everyone going into the building and then settled down to monitor everything.

One female visitor stayed in the building for about half an hour before leaving and heading across the car park to another office set up nearby. She repeated this operation three times – out of one office, across to my target's building and then back. When she made the final return trip she was carrying a briefcase that was identical to the one I had seen earlier. I wondered if it was more than just a coincidence, particularly when, at the end of the day, my target came out of the building and headed to her car without a briefcase.

I decided to return to the car park and take a look at the other woman. It might, I thought, be a wild goose chase, but I was in Milton Keynes anyway and I thought I'd give it a whirl. When she left her office, she too got in a brand-spanking-new, black BMW and was again carrying the briefcase that I had seen earlier. I was very intrigued.

I followed her, watched her park up and enter her home, only half a mile away from the main target. Recycling was being collected the following day and her bins were out and easily accessible. I waited until it began to get darker before helping myself to paperwork and envelopes in her recycling container. I threw them into the back of my car and headed to the main target's house and did the same there, swiftly grabbing whatever paperwork I could and stashing it in the boot of my car before returning to my hotel. I told Mark there was not much going on – the target would just drive to and from work. Sometimes I could see her in a café on the ground floor, at break and lunch times. Occasionally she had appeared with other members of staff.

I sorted through the paperwork, filtering out junk mail and concentrating on bank statements, telephone call records and business information from Companies House. Pages had been torn into quarters, but it was extremely easy to read when put back together, basically like a large jigsaw. Mark and I agreed that I'd leave it a week before going back to do the 'bin spin' again. In the meantime, I would study the paperwork further and do some research via HM Land Registry, Companies House and run the numbers through my database to see what I could find out. He was happy for me to do this.

Looking through photographs I found among the trawl, it was evident that the two women were quite similar in looks; it intrigued me. Could they be related? It wasn't obvious from their names as my main target was married and the second woman was single. When I next spoke to Mark he pulled out the first target's personnel file and confirmed that her maiden name was the same as the second woman's – and it wasn't a common name. This had to be much more than a mere coincidence: both were listed at Companies House as directors and both were running agency recruitment offices. I was certain they were sisters and I could see that the younger (who was the second woman I'd followed) had formed her company only four months previously; around the same time as my target's company had started showing problems.

I returned to Milton Keynes the following week and decided to lift paperwork from their houses and their offices as well. I took some black bin liners to hold the documents. I managed to get loads more paperwork, including records of telephone calls, bank transactions, client lists and company information. What it revealed was damning. We untangled the paper trail to show that the target woman had financed her sister's agency in plain sight – literally across the road in the second office. Client names on the target's roster appeared as customers of her sister's company and, unbelievably, she had also used her firm to furnish the second company with office stationery and equipment. When a courier would attempt to make delivery to her address, she would simply redirect them across the car park. Mark's venture capital company was unknowingly financing this sneaky start-up. It wasn't at all clear to me how she thought she would get away with it: all this double-accounting and the acquisition process would have shown up the moment the accounts were audited by the Manchester headquarters.

I was not sure that Mark could use my information as, strictly speaking, it was bordering on the illegal to take people's rubbish (although it's standard practice for private detectives to amass evidence this way). An ex-CID police officer mate advised me to get around the law by photocopying the original documents and returning the originals back to the bins. Mark invited me to Manchester with the copied paperwork. I thought to myself, *This is a right old can of worms I'm about to open in front of him in his own office.* I taped together the paperwork and put the copies in a file.

Mark decided to show the evidence to the company solicitor, but tell him it had arrived anonymously. He thought he would say something like the file could have been sent by a disgruntled member of the company in Milton Keynes. To make the story seem genuine, I was to take the folder back to Milton Keynes and post it to him by special delivery, personally signed for by him.

Some months later I learned about the results of the investigation. Based on the evidence and information gathered, Mark had managed to get what was termed an Anton Piller order served on the target's home and her sister's office. This was only granted in extreme circumstances and facilitated entry to an office or property where there was strong evidence that the respondent was guilty of possessing documents that they might well destroy if they had prior warning of a court case. Mark asked me to carry out a few days' surveillance just to confirm their daily routines. The sisters were very much continuing with business as usual. Mark had also taken out a Mareva injunction on both sisters, which would freeze their assets. They were about to get a hell of a shock. It was a strong combination – if they refused entry based on the Anton Piller order, they would be in contempt of court and could be arrested.

Mark was permitted legal access to my target's sister's company premises, the target's garage and her home office. I was there when the order was served. After I met Mark in the car park of my hotel, along with his two solicitors and his finance director, he took one solicitor to search the target's garage and home office, while the finance director accompanied the other solicitor to enter the sister's office at precisely the same time. The search took a few hours, during which time the men removed a load of documents and printed off a stack of information from the office computers. Mark and his finance director also visited the target's office – as he was the joint venture capital investor he did not need permission. Apparently, my former target was in a hell of a state because her sister had already rung her to tell her what was going on at her office. She had been making up all sorts of excuses and lies to which Mark responded with those immortal words, 'I'll see you in court.'

They did next meet in court, when the target was bankrupted and had to sell her house and cars and she split up from her husband. She was also dismissed as a company director. Her sister was also ordered to pay a vast amount of money to Mark's company in compensation – in excess of one million pounds to cover the loss of business. It was this that completely wiped out the sisters' assets and also meant that what they had done was now in the public domain. Their greed and conniving had pretty much been their ultimate downfall.

Mark hosted a conference in Manchester for all the managers and directors of his connected companies. He told them what had been going on; basically, he was firing a warning shot to warn key personnel that if anybody was engaged in underhand practices, they would get caught and they would suffer the same consequences.

Mark was impressed enough by my work to give me another task, this time in Swansea. A director he had funded had decided to leave the recruitment industry and sold her shares in her firm to Mark's parent company. She signed a contract that prevented her opening a similar outfit for six months and that agreement still had three months to go, but Mark had got the impression she would probably start up somewhere else. I was asked to put her under surveillance. I booked into a Swansea hotel that was just a short distance from her house. I thought I might possibly get a lucky dip in her recycling but there was nothing out that evening.

The next morning she drove into Swansea town, parked up and entered an office. I had already done a check on Companies House and knew that she had formed another company. The office had been decked out with her own livery and she had her new company name embossed on the window and door. That said, she was dressed down in a scruffy way that didn't fit in with office work – and particularly not in the recruitment world. I did a walk-past of the office and saw her and another woman painting and cleaning the place. Pretty much no work was going on in there; they were just setting up. Mark said to leave the job for a while and maybe go back in a couple of weeks. There was, he said, still time for her to breach the terms of her agreement.

When I returned the office was pretty much up and running, filled with computers, desks and all the things you would expect to see in a business – except employees. I saw the woman at her home address and followed her out, only to find she was only doing her shopping. Her six-month compliance contract soon finished and the following day she started her business: she had obviously decided to play by the rules. As for me, I got home to find two speeding fines in the post, both from Milton Keynes and both issued on the same day along different avenues. Six points and two hundred pounds worth of fines. Bugger.

Mark was a member of a business breakfast club and as part of his extensive networking he introduced me to a hair studio – one with a difference. They did hair transplanting and had a lot of celebrities on their books, Graham Gooch being among a load of cricket players who provided advertising, alongside football and rugby players. The studio had a problem similar to the one I'd encountered on my last job. They trained people at their various branches, hoping that they would work for them when they'd qualified. They were dismayed to find increasing numbers of fully trained staff quitting once they'd completed their apprenticeships. The owner incorporated a clause into their contracts that stopped them setting up on their own for six months or from having a similar business within a certain distance of the main headquarters. They also couldn't use a similar company name.

These clauses meant it would be pretty stupid to try and get away with breaking the contract. And yet, even so, my investigations unearthed two illicit competitors, one of them only about five hundred yards away from the main headquarters. She was threatened with court and closed down her business.

Alongside breach of contract surveillance tasks, I was involved with a number of close protection jobs that gave me the opportunity to meet blokes from varying backgrounds. Most were ex-servicemen and had amusing stories to relate both about their time in the military and as bodyguards. My mate Malcolm told me about the time he had been doing close protection for one of two notorious brothers in the music industry who had a bit of a reputation as hardmen. Malcolm was accompanying one of the brothers in a pub in Notting Hill, London. His charge went to the toilet and

Malcolm came back from the bar to see him emerge, his nose bleeding, his face in his hands. Someone had followed him in and had given him a decent pasting. Malcolm, berated for not protecting the brother, told him that he had deserved it and resigned on the spot. Malcolm told me later that although he was a very professional and committed security advisor, this particular bloke got what was coming to him, he could not stand him.

Another new friend who took himself off a similar job was John 'Tankie' Ross, an ex-member of the Royal Tank Regiment and the SAS. He had been looking after a self-promoting couple, a lord and lady who were obsessed with their own image. Their Chelsea-based team would be tasked with visiting the local newspaper shop daily to buy every paper and skim through each page to see if there were any articles about their employers. The couple would get quite annoyed if they had not been featured anywhere. When it was John's turn, he duly picked up every newspaper and laid them out on a table back at the house with the change. Her ladyship proceeded to count the change and accuse John of keeping a grand total of seven pence. He told her she could shove her job where the sun did not shine.

John also had a few funny stories about his time in the SAS; in particular, one exercise in which his troop had been parachuted into Germany to act out being sent behind enemy lines. But the drop was made in the wrong place and instead of being ensconced in a wooded area on the outskirts of a city, they landed in a small copse within a town. They camouflaged as best as they could but in the morning, as schools were starting, loads of German school kids wandered past saying, 'Guten Morgen, Britischer Soldat.' How embarrassing.

On another occasion his troop were required to carry out a reactive operation – or ambush – in Northern Ireland. Back in those days contact was made by using pagers and, even though his entire troop had been issued with the devices, headquarters could not get any reply to their order to initiate the action. It transpired that the whole troop was at a Def Leppard concert in Belfast and nobody had heard the pagers or felt them vibrate over the racket from the band. Funny as hell. They were all fined a substantial amount on their return to duty.

TEN

Most of the surveillance and close-protection tasks I carried out were based in the UK, but I did get some foreign postings.

During my time in the private investigation industry, I travelled to Washington, USA; Toronto, Canada; Kingston, Jamaica; Nicosia, Cyprus and Belgrade in the former Yugoslavia, to name but a few. All fascinating places under normal circumstances. However, I went to these places on work and only got the occasional day off to do the tourist thing.

One of my first ventures abroad was to Istanbul, Turkey, on a task that I would not generally have got involved in – repossessing a car. In this case it was a Porsche 911 belonging to a London-based company that I had to drive back to London. It was quite an adventure. The Mayfair-based company had kitted out a large number of their employees with these luxury icons – they had very high standards indeed. When one of their representatives decided to quit the company he returned home to Istanbul ... taking his company car with him!

I flew to Istanbul armed only with the former employee's name, the vehicle details, and a set of spare keys. I contacted a friend of a friend, Brian, who would assist me with local knowledge and translation and made contact with him on my arrival. We met at the famous Pera Palace hotel, where it was said that Agatha Christie wrote *Murder on the Orient Express*. Brian was a former Met officer whose wife was Turkish and he had retired to the capital where they ran a small domestic company supplying cleaners to local businesses. He knew the area well and was only too happy to help me in my quest.

The first hitch was my target's surname – Yilmaz. Brian told me that it was the most common name in the whole country and the first name, he went on, was not much less popular. In other words, I was doing the equivalent of searching for 'David Jones' in Wales. Not a good start. In any case, he said, Istanbul had no electoral roll or citizen database. The only option was to go to the post office and search the telephone directory there – but I had to be prepared for disappointment when I saw how many people were listed with that surname.

My challenges didn't stop with finding my quarry. It might not be easy to drive out of the country, warned Brian, adding that it wouldn't be enough to have the spare keys, a letter of authority from the owners and a copy of the vehicle's documents. Brian raised the unwelcome possibility that, in a dispute about ownership, the border police would side with their own national, stop me and impound the vehicle. Not only might they return the car to the thief, they could even arrest me. I decided I would give it a go anyway.

The following day I made my way to the post office on what I was already sure would be a pointless mission and was amazed to find that the telephone directory was just a load of loose sheets in no particular order and anyway inadequate in content. I told my employers and they agreed to me staying in Istanbul for a few days just on the off-chance that I might make any headway.

I did the tourist thing and wandered around the capital, venturing out of the main part of the city to the Bosphorus, the narrow strip of water that forms a division between east and west, with Europe on one side of the water and Asia on the other. I sat on a wall and took out a can of cold drink, my contemplation abruptly disturbed by the unmistakable sound of a Porsche 911 roaring its way up the road. I couldn't believe it. The car I was looking for drove straight past. I sprinted to a telephone box and rang Brian, describing the area and attempting to spell out the road names. Brian was ecstatic – from my description he was able to tell that the car was headed out to a peninsula. He said, 'You've got him.' Porsche-thief was heading to a new complex of upmarket flats, very much the Istanbul yuppie district.

Meanwhile, Brian had been making inquiries with his contacts and had discovered that Yilmaz had re-registered the car. To all intents and purposes it was now his property and, if it vanished, he could report it stolen and I would be in a lot of trouble if I was caught with it. This was a crazy situation. I rang the client in Mayfair and explained; they were as amazed as I was. We discussed some options as they, furious, wanted to let Yilmaz know where they stood in principle and to spell out that he wasn't going to get away with it. They floated some wild questions – would I be prepared to burn the vehicle? No. Would I take it and dump it in the sea? Out of the question.

We got nowhere and it seemed we were out of ideas. Even so, I made my way down to the flats and swiftly located the car. As I took stock of the situation Yilmaz himself appeared from nearby and approached the vehicle. What did I have to lose? I immediately said, 'Hello,' and he looked very shocked at the sound of an English voice. I didn't have any cards to play and I simply told him upfront exactly why I was there. He looked shaken again, and I held my poker face. I was aware, I said, that he had re-registered the car and I pretended not to be concerned by his move, bluffing that it didn't make any difference as he had 'stolen' the car in London. I was there to take the car back. Then the twist came.

He asked how much I was getting paid for the job, suggesting that if he paid the same amount, would I let him keep the car? I told him I would think about it and would return later that day. I warned that if he reneged on the idea I would bide my time and he could be sure I would return for the vehicle. He agreed.

I headed off to call the client; they agreed that, given all the likely problems in trying to take the vehicle, I could do the deal and take him for as much as I could. We went together to a bank in Istanbul. While I waited in the car he went and withdrew the cash, handed it over and we parted ways. An interesting and profitable little jaunt, even if it hadn't gone quite the way I'd have wanted.

One slight mishap did occur while I was in Istanbul but it turned out better than it might have done. After dinner one night I was having a few beers in a bar in the main part of town; it was very busy and bustling, as you would expect in a Turkish city. I was on my way back to my hotel when a bloke appeared in front of me, blocking my way and pointing a pistol in my face. Not the nicest of endings to my evening. He wanted my wallet and facing down his barrel was quite an incentive for me to do as he told me. He dashed off without checking the contents, but I knew he would be disappointed when he did. Five lira (about fifty pence), a couple of out-of-date credit cards – their chips scratched with a knife – and a few taxi-driver business cards from the hotel. Thanks to a tip a colleague gave me before I left London, the mugger was the mug: he had my dummy wallet, carefully stashed in the front right-hand pocket of my jeans. The real one was still safely in my back pocket. I can recommend that approach if you are ever considering taking a trip to a city with a reputation.

My next venture came with its own share of surprises. I was tasked with carrying out surveillance on behalf of a client in Chelsea and my colleague, Ted, and I followed the target's car from his driveway all the way to the M4 motorway. Our brief was to keep tailing him no matter where he went. We had one car each and, working as we were on a busy Friday evening without backup, this was a real test. We stayed with him until he hit the M25, when he headed south to the M3 exit, the motorway heading south-west, well away from London. He just kept going and going and he was driving fast, too. We were really pushed to keep with him, but we did and – just over five hours and nearly three hundred miles later – we reached the outskirts of Penzance at the far end of Cornwall. He turned into a country house in an area called Longrock. This was the longest follow I had ever done and we were well chuffed at having made it. We were somewhat deflated when the client told Ted that he had suspected this is where the target would be heading; I could not believe he had not let us know that beforehand but at least we had completed the task – or so we thought.

The client knew that our target was due to go to Toronto, Canada, and instructed us to continue the surveillance. I always carried my passport on jobs and kept a kitbag in the boot of my car with enough gear for a few days. Ted had a contact in Toronto who would join us and the client agreed to the extra body on the job. The following day Ted and I were met by his mate at the airport, complete with two hire cars, two mobile phones and a booking at an airport hotel. Good skills all round.

In the evening we waited for the target to land and, as soon as I picked him up on foot in arrivals, I followed to the pick-up area before calling Ted and his mate to let them know what car he was using. They took on the target while I picked up my hire car.

Our man was dropped off at one of the Hilton hotels in the airport area. Ted called the client who – in a massive twist – declared that the job was now complete and that we should cease surveillance. This was bonkers. We headed to our hotel to have a few beers and decide what to do next. Ted suggested we that we stay a few days and settled on playing golf with a mate at a Niagara Falls club the following day. As a non-golfer, I opted to surprise an old school mate, Greg, who now lived in the area.

Greg and I had been mates since we were five and went to school together. He served a couple of years in the same regiment as me, went on a holiday to Spain and met a Canadian girl. Next I heard from him, he had moved to Toronto for good. Although we didn't see each other much, we still exchanged Christmas cards and every now and again we would talk on the phone. Now, I drove to his street, parked directly outside his house and called his landline. Success – he was in: this was going to be a laugh. Midway through our catch-up conversation he asked 'Where are you these days?'

He laughed when I replied, 'Outside your house', but I saw him looking out of the window.

Staying commendably understated, he said, 'You'd better come in, then.'

The next twenty-four hours we had a complete blast, catching up on old times and getting completely smashed on beer and Irish whiskey. We even gave a rendition of our old school song. Eventually, I headed back to the airport and flew home to await my next task.

It was another trip abroad. 'Fancy a week's work in Belgrade?' I knew that the city was the capital of what was then war-torn Yugoslavia and that the whole of the country was a very dangerous and dodgy place and in the complete turmoil of the Kosovo War. I pondered for a moment what it might mean before saying that I was available. I went to London for my briefing.

In the chaos of conflict, sanctions had limited goods going into the country, but the UN alleged that Sony was in breach of the regulations. Their goods were said to be openly on sale. A group of us were to buy any Sony products we could find, take photographs of the serial numbers and barcodes and then destroy the items. Sony would then find out where the goods were being made and how they were being distributed.

I was working with an ex-SAS guy I knew and an ex-bomb disposal officer I'd not met – both were good blokes. We decided that the best way to get into the capital was to fly to Budapest, Hungary, stay one night and take an eight-hour train journey through the country directly to Belgrade: what could possibly go wrong?

The train was very reminiscent of war movies, the scenes in which the Gestapo walk down the corridor, open the

118

compartment door and demand to see everyone's papers and passes. It had a buffet car that sold hard bread, cheese and bottles of beer that were ten years out of date. I'd pop the cap and literally have to spoon out the yeast that had formed on the top. Still, I told myself ... it was better than nothing.

We rumbled along for four hours, when the train came to a halt at the border between Hungary and what was then Yugoslavia, near the town of Subotica, now in Serbia. The crew and staff all changed around here as the train was handed over to a Yugoslavian team; we sat, looking out of the window at the employees milling about, signing documents and handing over pieces of equipment. The door to our carriage slid open quickly and two men – not Gestapo, fortunately, but dressed in long, black leather overcoats – stood in the doorway and announced, 'Passports.'

I handed over my document with a sinking feeling: it had been issued to me when I serving in Cyprus. I'd had to get back to the UK for a funeral and, to speed up the process, the British consulate in Nicosia had used a uniformed photo, complete with collar badges. This might not go down too well in wartime. British mercenaries were swarming towards the fighting and some were being arrested and jailed on the way. My heart pounded. One of guards pointed at my photograph and made a gesture that I did not really understand. Just then, a railway employee walked past the window. His uniform had collar badges and epaulettes and I pointed him out to indicate as best I could that I was a railway employee back home. The guard nodded, stamped my passport and handed it back. He checked the other two and then left, at which point the ex-SAS bloke – who had picked up on my panic, smirked and said, 'Do you need the toilet?'

At our hotel, we got sorted out and headed to the bar where we were at least able to get beers that were in date. The Yugoslavian dinar was in drastic trouble and everyone we came across would only accept dollars, sterling or deutschmarks, which was fine as we had taken loads of sterling to buy any Sony goods we could get our hands on. We decided to go for a wander around the area and see what we could find. We were constantly hassled for '*Novac, novac*, visa, visa,' '*novac*' being Croatian for 'money' and meaning, basically, any currency other than the person's own. We tried a bureau de change and as we were stood in the office we could watch the dinar devaluing in real time; it was a quite extraordinary sight.

The following day we easily found Sony products at a market stall, just a few yards away from our hotel. We decided to look for more outlets, split up to purchase different items as individuals and then rendezvous to the hotel. When we all got together again we had managed to purchase a mobile phone, a fax machine and a portable photocopier, all Sony and all sold on the black market quite openly. We continued in the same vein the next day, this time finding new market stalls to make similar purchases and returning to the hotel to take photographs of the items, their barcodes, any shipping information and the boxes. All the items were USA-manufactured and registered in the States too. We paused for a non-shopping day; we didn't want to arouse too much interest by hiking up the number of purchases of Sony illicit goods too quickly in one area. We decided to make our final purchases on the same day we headed back to Budapest.

That evening we got into a conversation with some locals at the bar and, while we didn't reveal too much about the purpose of our visit, we were able to tease out some useful information. It became evident that organised crime gangs were responsible for all goods sold on the market stalls, not just Sony gear. The mafia had an iron grip on everything imported via Romania and Bulgaria and then shipped up the Danube River and into Belgrade. Nobody dared intervene and even the authorities had no control over the gangs. Sony themselves were not in any way connected with these imports and were pretty helpless to stop it.

We made our final purchases, recorded the details and made for the railway station. We cut wires inside our electrical purchases to make them unworkable and left them in a cleaner's cupboard on our hotel corridor. Who knows, after we left, maybe a lucky cleaner got them repaired? There were a lot of valuable items in our haul of illicit goods. As we got on the train for our return journey I was able to make passport control a little easier. I had a second passport with a photo of me in civilian dress and I made sure that was handy and the other was hidden away.

One of the strangest jobs I ever did was in Washington DC. I received a call from Nigel, a contact who had a bit of a reputation for providing quite interesting jobs; he was very wealthy and a bit of a wild card. He asked me if I fancied a trip to the USA to try and get some information on behalf of a Saudi Arabian client. We would fly to Paris where he would meet his client and then on to Washington. All first class. One stipulation was that I had to bring my press card with me, which I had acquired after writing *Fishers of Men*. I wrote some newspaper articles and this qualified me to become a member of the British Association of Journalists.

We took his Aston Martin to the airport and straight into first-class, valet parking and into the terminal. On arrival in Paris, he left me in the terminal and disappeared for about two hours. He said that we were to try and get into any of the state department offices and gain as much information that the US had on a character by the name of Osama bin Laden. At the time I had no idea who bin Laden was, as this was about three years prior to bin Laden becoming internationally known due to his organising of the attack on the World Trade Center on 11 September 2001. We flew in luxury to Washington and to the Jefferson hotel, a seriously decadent and expensive establishment.

The next day we went to the state department to try and make an appointment under their freedom of information rules to gain information on what US interest there was in bin Laden. We expected to be rebuffed but, acting as investigative journalists, we were given an appointment for the following day. We took the rest of the day to do some sight-seeing and that evening we ate at the Rare Steakhouse restaurant, possibly the city's most expensive place to eat. Nigel was also a bit of a wine connoisseur and very rarely drank anything that did not cost around one hundred pounds a bottle.

We returned to the state department for our interview and were seen immediately by an officer who dealt with Middle Eastern affairs. He was not forthcoming with any information regarding our inquiry – following the later attacks of 9/11 in New York, hindsight obviously explains why well enough. We left the department with pretty much nothing and, back at the hotel, Nigel went off to his room to call his client. His client gave him an address to follow up in Cape Cod and he said he needed me to go and take some photographs of a property. At least, that was his story. I could stay there for a couple of days if I fancied, he said, and then we would both head back to London via Washington. It was all a bit surreal, quite strange and to this day I do think he wanted me out of the way for some unknown reason but off to the airport I headed. I took the photos as requested and also managed to get a tour of Martha's Vineyard as well: it had always intrigued me and now was the perfect time to go. I wasn't sure what Nigel got up to while I was away but when we returned to London he had a folder with him that he did not arrive with and he was very clearly not going to tell me what was in it.

On the flight back to Paris he asked if I wanted to go to Nicosia, Cyprus, to photograph another property. During my absence, he explained, he had been to the Saudi Arabian embassy for a meeting with his client. I was still not sure what was going on and why this new task had been introduced but I was free and was soon back on a plane with him and on my way to Nicosia. We stayed in central Nicosia and, just as in the United States, I went off to photograph the property alone after Nigel told me that he had a meeting to attend; all quite strange, to say the least. I guessed that he went off to the Saudi embassy in Nicosia. We stayed in Cyprus for two more days – doing nothing in particular – before heading home. But that wasn't the end of it. On the return flight, Nigel asked if I would undertake another photographic task, this time in Kingston, Jamaica. I was to fly to Dallas, Texas, and stay with a mutual friend in the Fort Worth area, wait for another acquaintance to join me and then we would both go to Jamaica. Nigel was not coming on this trip as he claimed he had some other business. My mind boggled.

Landing at Dallas was delayed due to a massive electrical storm in the area, as a result of which the plane took up a figure-of-eight holding pattern. Although this was a bit of a nuisance, the pilot tilted the aircraft from left to right so that all of us could watch the storm; it was a truly amazing experience to be watching a lightning display thousands of feet below and I had never seen such an epic display of Mother Nature's power. In the end, we had to divert to Houston, refuel and fly back to Dallas. By the time we returned, the storm had moved on and we were able to land – eight hours late. I was picked up at the airport by Robbie, an ex-CIA operative who I had met on several occasions in London.

As well as working in the investigations business, Robbie was a real Texas cowboy and I never saw him without his ten-gallon hat. He invited me to go and stay at his ranch in the southern area of the state. He told me that he had no internet or telephone at his residence and he also did not own a television. What he did have, he said, was a thousand head of beef cattle, a fridge full of cold beer and twelve quarter horses – these got their name, he explained, from their ability to gallop extremely quickly for about a quarter of a mile before having to rest. They were perfectly suited to rounding up cattle. His father looked after the ranch when he was away.

Robbie had been waiting patiently in the bar for me to land and in the eight hours I was delayed he had managed to get hilariously drunk. He had to hand me the keys to his pickup truck and just about pointed out where it was parked. It was somewhat daunting – I had not driven on the right-hand side of the road for a long time and his truck was massive in a typically Texan way. Two hunting rifles perched on a gun rack behind the front seats, on display for all to see. Texans love their second amendment – the right to bear arms – even more than they love their big trucks.

We headed out to Fort Worth and to the house owned by Gareth, another ex-CIA operative. It was great to be meeting up with both men again. I stayed in Gareth's place for a few days and did a bit of touring around with him. His registration plates showed that he was a sponsor of both the Purple Heart foundation, which supports military veterans, and the Dallas police widows' fund. I asked how he came to choose these two and he grinned, 'I don't get any parking tickets in this city.' Fair enough.

In fact, both Robbie and Gareth had served in the US army in Vietnam and both had been members of the famous 101st Airborne Division, the 'Screaming Eagles'. They had seen heavy combat in the country and were part of the elite Tiger Force, a long-range reconnaissance unit that would go deep into enemy territory to cause havoc. Tiger Force would later be accused of war crimes and also killed over a thousand Viet Cong soldiers. Both men became enforcement officers on the border between Texas and Mexico before joining the CIA.

Robbie and I flew to Jamaica via Florida and, as we were to stay there for a few days, we took the opportunity to do a bit of wandering around Kingston. It was a bit of a culture shock, a really rough place with loads of people hassling us to become our tour guides. All claimed to be related to Bob Marley and promised they could take us to all the places where Marley was known to have been. We declined and retreated to the relative luxury of our hotel. That evening we decided to visit a nearby hotel that had a promising happy hour. Robbie and I were wandering towards the outer gates of our hotel when the concierge came running after us, shouting at us to stop. He explained that we should wait for the hotel minibus to take us and that when we wanted to return we should call him to arrange transport. It was only a hundred yards and we were a bit baffled by his outburst and even more so when the minibus turned up with a guard armed with a pump-action shotgun! The concierge explained that even the short journey between two hotels was risky at night. Two white tourists on that road would definitely be mugged. We took up the offer of the thirty-second drive.

The job was simple. We located the property and took the photographs that were requested and headed back to the airport for the flight to Dallas. I was going to stay with Gareth for a few more days before returning to the UK. I was surprised when the Kingston American Airlines staff asked me to produce my onward flight tickets from Dallas to London. My ticket was sitting at Robbie's place in the US, I explained, but it was no use. The only way I could get on the plane was by purchasing a new onward ticket at Kingston, which luckily I was able to get refunded when I arrived in Dallas.

Robbie and I arrived back at Fort Worth, only to be told we were not welcome at Gareth's house that evening. He and his son had gone away bird-shooting and his teenage daughter was having a load of her friends around for a sleepover. We dropped off our bags and spent the night at a country-and-western bar for cowboys in Dallas until breakfast time. It was a great night.

ELEVEN

Somalia is located on the eastern coast of Africa, nestled between Kenya to the south and Ethiopia to the west, with the small country of Djibouti making up the third border to the north-west tip of the country.

The Gulf of Aden flows out into the Arabian Sea to its north and then into the Indian Ocean along the northern and eastern sides. It had become a lawless country with pirates targeting ships in the area. Gangsters knew that that prosperous shipping companies would pay massive ransoms to release their cargos and crews. It was a thriving business, the gangsters having access to many young, drug-fuelled, desperate Somalis who could be made to risk their lives for carrying out the raids.

Around the middle of 2009, Graham and I had decided that we would get into the business of maritime security; it was a growing industry with these ungovernable terrorists of Somalia in de facto charge of the longest coastline of Africa's mainland. We distributed a brochure detailing the services we could provide for protecting the massive tankers that were being regularly attacked in that region. The main targets for our campaign were the commercial shipping giants, but we also reached out to the super-yacht industry as well – a number of these had been attacked and in some cases hostages had been taken from the yachts. We had the resources to handle any complex kidnap and ransom situation and we could also provide a specialist marine surveying package.

We teamed up with a contact that Graham had met in Spain, Ray, a regional crime squad police officer who had been involved in anti-terrorist operations for many years. He specialised in the maritime industry, particularly yachts, although he also had vast knowledge of commercial ship operations in the Greek shipping industry; he could speak Greek fluently, which was a massive bonus. We were also joined by an ex-warrant officer from the Special Boat Service (SBS), the Royal Navy equivalent of the SAS. He had been a commando with the Royal Marines and was easily one of the best soldiers I had ever known. He had achieved a rare feat in transferring to the SAS from the SBS. He had to find a sponsoring regiment and went for the Parachute Regiment, who insisted that he must pass their own gruelling selection process run by their P Company. Having managed that, he immediately went on to pass the SAS selection as well. I have never heard of anyone else achieving this. His areas for us were training, planning and briefing and procurement of specialised equipment. He had experience of giving safe passage to a number of super yachts on journeys through the Gulf of Aden and had been involved in successfully repelling pirate attacks. He was a very experienced trainer and instructor. Alongside our main team were standby members who would fill in if anyone was unable to travel to the Gulf region.

The majority of our manpower for these tasks were going to be either ex-marines or ex-navy but we did have a number of retired soldiers amongst the team who had particular talents. We set up a training course that was to be run at Weymouth on the south coast of the UK and sourced a former member of the army's Physical Training Corps who ran a maritime survival centre and also a pub. That meant he could provide accommodation and meals – it was a good pub – along with all the facilities that were required for training, all in one location: it was ideal.

We decided that it would only be fair that Graham, Ray and I also went through the training course as well. The course was not going to be easy: the majority of our line-up was made up of extremely fit, younger blokes, while the management – a.k.a. the three amigos – were middle-aged with ever-increasing waistlines. We all had to undergo various lessons in physical maritime navigation, nautical radio procedures, sea survival, life-raft control, unarmed combat, maritime attack early-warning procedures, command post-control and liaison techniques with both terrorists and government agencies.

At the end of the course we had official qualifications in every aspect of the course and I ached like hell for weeks after. The only phase I was excused from was resistance to interrogation and physical interrogation itself, as I had already been through these particular sections when I completed selection for special duties many years previously. This style of training is a realistic experience and it only really works once; once you know what's likely to happen the lack of surprise renders it minimally useful. Instead, I assisted the instructor (and it was pretty good fun to be on the other side).

The fact that Graham, Ray and I took the course went down well with the students. They were full of respect for us and it was good to have that bond with the people who were going to be working with us.

We were soon approached by our first client, the extremely wealthy owner of a super yacht worth millions of pounds. He wanted to sail south through the Suez Canal and on to the Seychelles, where he planned to spend some months scuba diving. The route would take him past Somalia to the west and he was concerned about the possibility of being attacked and kidnapped by pirates. He was right to consider it – the risk and the threat were very real and he could be a sitting duck.

Graham was in contact with an arms dealer in Malta who would provide weapons and ammunition for our team when they called into Djibouti, neighbouring Somali. He was a licensed trader and provided all the necessary paperwork and end-user certificates. It was more tricky on the return journey, as to take semi-automatic machine guns back through the Suez was illegal. The only way to get around it was to jettison the weaponry into the sea past Somalia on the way back. This was very lucrative for our Maltese dealer, as we'd then have to order another batch for the next job. Various backhanders also had to be arranged for the harbour master at a Djibouti port in the Gulf of Tadjoura.

Our team of four flew to Cairo, Egypt, and then travelled by car to Port Said to join the super yacht. They sailed through the Gulf of Suez and brought the weaponry and ammunition on board as arranged with the harbour master in Djibouti. The client was apparently quite freaked out by the fact that all the team were now armed to the teeth and I was told he spent most of the journey hiding in his cabin. But the journey went well and was luckily without incident. The team flew back from the island of Mahé in the Seychelles. Our first job was complete.

Ray was already in talks with a Greek shipping company; they had asked that he visit them to discuss our providing security for one of their bigger ships. The business was becoming quite serious now and we were delighted to be getting ourselves in front of some of the biggest maritime companies in the world. They did need help: the problems for ocean-going ships using the Suez Canal were getting worse and the pirates were becoming more dangerous, with attacks taking place almost on a daily basis. Insurance companies were beginning to tell their clients that they had to have security on board if they were near Somalia or their cover would be invalid. Great news for us – obviously not so good for the shipping companies.

The Greek company was sending one of its massive wheat carriers down through the Suez Canal and out into the Indian Ocean via the Gulf of Aden. They wanted our team to be onboard – and they wanted them armed. We decided to adopt the same routine as we'd used with the team who carried out the super-yacht job, and the next team also sourced their weapons and ammunition at Djibouti. This team took extra precautions with the ship as well, taking out the rear climbing ladder and covering both sides of the ship with barbed wire entanglements that dangled down from the decks. This was to combat the grappling hooks that the pirates had taken to chucking up on their targets. They would lock in and rope-climb their way on board (very much like the very earliest pirates). At certain points on a ship there were staging points where, once successful in getting a grappling hook in position, pirates could clamber up the side. On the wheat carrier, these areas were all soaked in slippery engine oil. Our ship had very high-power fire extinguishers that looked more like anti-aircraft guns and these were noted in case they could be turned to face the sea as opposed to the contents.

As the ship cruised about one hundred miles off the coastlines of Yemen and Oman, three pirate boats were spotted in the distance, headed directly for the Greek wheat carrier. The Somali pirates had instigated a new tactic that involved using a large mothership to carry smaller skiffs for their raids. Our group knew that the pirates would be drunk, as they invariably were, and stoned out of their heads on hallucinatory drugs, making them totally fearless and much more dangerous. Our protection team got every member of the crew into a safe area of the ship known as the 'citadel' and only the captain remained on the bridge with our men. He sent out a distress message.

As the three skiffs closed in on the ship, the guys on board our vessel could see through their binoculars that the pirates were carrying a variety of weapons and were brandishing them wildly, waving guns that included AK-47s while – rather more worryingly for the watchers – it appeared that at least two of the pirates were carrying rocket-propelled grenade-launchers. The team came to stand to status, all armed with semi-automatic machine guns and loads of ammunition. They also wore Kevlar bulletproof jackets and helmets. They pointed their weapons at the fast-approaching pirates until the order to fire was given by the team leader and the pirate skiffs were hit by a volley of rounds fired at an extremely fast rate.

There were a few returning bursts of fire from the AK-47-wielding pirates and a rocket-propelled grenade was launched towards the ship. It scored a direct hit on one side of the ship's bridge but, thankfully, nobody was injured. In the distance, two naval frigates were spotted heading to the area, the captain's distress call having been heard by sailors from a joint German and Turkish naval patrol that was carrying out routine anti-piracy manoeuvres in the area. Two of the pirate skiffs retreated to their mothership while the third was trapped by the navy patrol frigates and boarded by teams of commandoes. They apprehended four or five of the pirates who were, true to form, stoned out of their heads.

The crew of the wheat carrier were allowed to resume their work stations while our team liaised with the German and Turkish crews. Graham received a report of events from our team leader and was also contacted by a Turkish reporter who was keen to get an update about how his country's navy had assisted in the rescue: he was after a good story about the whole event.

Even without the assistance of the navy, it was unlikely that the pirates would have been successful in their bid. Our team was hitting them with a fair amount of firepower and, as experienced former marines and army servicemen, they had all been in combat situations before. The outcome of the job proved to be a good advertisement for their services and more calls began to come from shipping companies inquiring about the provision of armed guards for their own ships in the region. News travelled fast, but then the Greek shipping empire was made up of family dynasties, lots of very wealthy brothers owning similar businesses.

At the same time, these fabulously wealthy Greek super tanker and freight ship-owners always seemed to want to strike a lower price bargain for our services, even though their future livelihoods depended on the protection of their assets. Funny that. As a result, although the team were paid decent-enough wages and we made some profit, it was far from a life-changing enterprise.

News was also travelling fast about the increasingly large number of pirate attacks taking place. It was a bit of an epidemic, with larger hijacked ships repurposed as motherships, while the pirates held their crews at gunpoint, forced to run the ships under threat of death. Ransom amounts were getting higher and the monsoon season was not slowing their violent activities as much as it normally did. Worst of all, the pirates were becoming more violent, young Somalis offered huge amounts of money by their gangmasters to take more ships. The gangsters were in turn making ludicrous amounts from the ransoms.

The Somali basin became home to numerous large tankers and ships with hundreds of crew members being held captive. The pirates had been quite professional in disabling the Automatic Identification System (AIS) that tracked every sea-going vessel. This had the effect of making a ship disappear off the satellite system and it was virtually impossible to follow where the stolen ships were taken. In one successful rescue operation, a South Korean tanker that had been seized by pirates was boarded by a team of commandoes that launched a bid to free the crew. Seven or eight pirates were shot dead during the fire fight.

Our team continued to travel back and forth to the Gulf region on many more missions until, as we'll find out later, that side of our business had to be closed down and we left the maritime protection industry.

TWELVE

The Mayfair-based company I worked with a lot asked me to go to the Costa del Sol, Spain, to carry out some anti-surveillance on behalf of celebrity underworld figure Ronnie Knight. He needed to know if he was being watched and, if so, I was to carry out some counter-surveillance. It was all pretty straightforward, really, I had been doing this kind of thing for years.

East-Ender Knight had been a close friend of Ronnie and Reggie Kray, the infamous twins who had ruled that part of London with a combination of violence and intimidation back in the sixties. He had been linked to a robbery at a Security Express depot for which his brother, John, had been arrested and was later to be sentenced to twenty-two years in prison. Ronnie himself fled the country and was now on the run in Spain. He had been a nightclub owner and had two properties on Charing Cross Road and Denmark Street, Soho, that were often frequented by criminals and gangland personalities along with celebrities. He notably married actor Barbara Windsor and they divorced in the mid-eighties.

Knight decided that he had been away from the UK for too long; he had been on the Costa del Sol for around ten years and wanted to return to his homeland. He had been having money problems and had made a deal with the *Sun* newspaper. Knight would give a full and detailed life story to a friend of ours, the features editor of the paper, in exchange for a substantial sum of money and also to arrange his transportation back home. We had been approached to provide security, hire a private jet for his return and secure his safe passage from Spain to a private airfield in the south of England.

Graham had contacts in the private jet industry and that was easily organised, the anti-surveillance task at his property was straightforward and everything was set to successfully repatriate Knight. The paper got their interview and he was driven to the airport at Malaga. Even private jets have to provide a manifest, a list of all passengers along with their dates of birth and passport details. These are submitted to HMRC before landing. As we knew he would be, one Ronald Knight, born on 20 January 1934, was instantly flagged up on the police national computer system as all the 'fugitive' sirens went off.

On landing at an airport near Farnborough it became obvious that a welcoming party from the Met was ready and waiting for his return. He was duly arrested and taken away by CID officers from Scotland Yard. He was later tried for his part in the Security Express robbery and was sentenced to seven years in prison for handling £300,000 of the estimated six million pounds that had been taken. But my company had played its part and everyone split up to wait for the next task. I did not have to hang around too long.

My business partner, Graham, had spent some time living in Spain and had made a number of really good contacts there. One of these was a chartered accountant, Richard Smith, who managed the accounts of some very dodgy ex-pats leading nice lifestyles while keeping their finances tucked out of sight of the UK's tax authorities. Richard was a number cruncher who knew how to handle a client's wealth.

Richard had been playing golf in Marbella with a shady character called Tom Hinton and, in their discussions, suggested that he might like to be introduced to Graham. Their meeting took place a few days later in a restaurant on the seafront at

Puerto Banus, one of Spain's upmarket areas with many super yachts parked up in the harbour. Tom had an investigation ready for us, a bit of digging around in the work of a financial adviser to ascertain if there were any skeletons in his cupboard. Graham came back to the UK and we met at our office on the outskirts of Towcester, Northamptonshire.

This was the first time that Graham mentioned Tom Hinton's name and he was surprised to hear that I already knew it. I had carried out an inquiry and tracing job on Hinton for an investigation company in Basingstoke. Their client was a solicitor who represented a consortium of about fifteen or sixteen people who had been ripped off by Hinton for around thirty-five million pounds. He had used a sophisticated property scam and then seemingly vanished off the face of the earth. What a coincidence to find him now! He was a nasty piece of work and typically the kind of criminal that we worked to bring to justice. Many of the people that Hinton had defrauded had lost their whole life savings and it would be very satisfying if we could get that money back.

The victims had been taken in by the world that Hinton created. He had set up a swish office on Curzon Street, Mayfair, a suitably prestigious W1 address in London, surrounded by salubrious offices and buildings boasting high-end businesses and shops. He had kitted the office out with fantastic leather furniture and had a team of beautiful women working the reception area. Tom himself would park his bright red Ferrari outside the main door to the office and was always a snappy dresser in expensive Savile Row suits. He was always one to make an entrance. He had the look of the high achiever and was absolutely charming in his manner.

The office was decorated with bespoke, beautifully framed prints of expensive Spanish villas. Elaborate blueprints and architects' drawings of yet more impressive Spanish villas sat on easels. Tom's business received much attention and he would hold invitation-only receptions for the great and good of Mayfair, his gorgeous receptionists dishing out ice-cold Moët & Chandon champagne to all. These events must have cost a small fortune to put together; it was all to impress and he certainly did that with some panache. He knew how to dangle a carrot – a gold-plated one at that – and he was equally proficient at getting people to part with their money: a consummate conman.

Tom Hinton weaved his magic by inviting, at his expense, his putative victims to travel business-class to Marbella where he provided chauffeur-driven limousines to take them to stay at the Marbella Club hotel, a well-known golf and spa resort, one of the top destinations in the area. Most of the people who had been at the sales-pitch evening attended. From there he had them driven in comfort to meet an 'architect' at the site of the lavish hillside resort illustrated in his office. The alleged architect himself was just one of Hinton's cronies who worked from a well-prepared script to add authenticity to what was a complete charade. A few unfortunates signed up for the promised homes there and then and others said they would get in touch in due course.

Hinton encouraged a steady stream of interested visitors to the hotel in Marbella over the course of a fortnight, telling each of his intention to have ten splendid villas built to sell for five to fifteen million pounds each. These dream homes would benefit, he promised, from dedicated resort security that would patrol the area twenty-four hours a day and although their properties would be impenetrable they would also include state-of-the-art security systems, with designated panic rooms for the owners. He set about helping his clients to organise large deposits and make bank transfers. He had very complex and elaborate contracts ready to sign at the hotel, where he discussed the way forward with some of the interested parties. It was a convincing sting. The clients all then flew back to the UK and, once he had gathered up a fortune from the deposits, he vanished.

The office in Curzon Street was emptied, all of the elegant displays and leather furniture gone. His phone number was now dead, without even a voicemail, and it was when they discovered this that the investors realised they had been totally and professionally scammed for a serious amount of money. It must have been a massive shock for all of them. The shop's managing agents told the solicitor representing the victims that Hinton had paid cash on a daily basis for the rental and there was no paper trail that could provide any clues as to his whereabouts. The freeholders were not that bothered by what had happened – they got their rent money.

I explained the whole sorry story to Graham, who managed to track down the solicitor, Helen. He asked her if she still had any interest in a certain gentleman by the name of Tom Hinton. She was more than keen to make his acquaintance again but would obviously have to seek permission from her roster of victims and see if they would be prepared to pay for an investigation into the man himself and to try and locate the funds that he had stolen. The account used to take the victims' money was located somewhere in the Turks and Caicos Island and all the deposits had later been moved twice, ending up in Switzerland where the cash was well-hidden due to the banking laws that provided anonymity there. Hinton had done his homework. But we had a man who could possibly help: Danny, whose profession was blagger. He could get information from all sorts of sources, including foreign banks.

Graham went to dinner with Hinton at Annabel's, the exclusive members' club in Berkeley Square, and discussed the work that Hinton wanted. In a way, this was a bit of a reverse sting on Hinton, keeping him engaged. I kept out of it, in case we wanted to put some surveillance on him at a later date. We would not want to compromise the task by allowing him to know who I was. Graham was fully briefed on the inquiry Hinton wanted us to carry out and a fee of eight thousand pounds had been agreed. He wanted a lot of sensitive information gathered on his financial advisor.

Graham had remained in loose contact with Richard, the accountant friend in Spain. He had been very scathing about

Hinton who, apparently, had not paid his account fees. Graham asked how much he was owed, and it turned out the balance of non-paid invoices amounted to eight thousand pounds – quite a coincidence. Graham asked Richard about Hinton's accounts and if was there any sensitive information that might be useful in an inquiry. There was. Apparently, Richard held a great deal of banking and property information on Hinton, including details of a few of his offshore accounts. Graham asked if he could make copies and he'd reimburse Richard for the eight thousand pounds that Hinton owed him. Richard, who had just been ripped off, readily agreed. Graham flew back to Spain and returned with full copies of Hinton's financial history. Here were the keys that Danny would be able to use to get the information we required.

In the meantime, we had been given the go-ahead from Helen, who had heard from her own clients. We could now start tracing the missing funds and we got together with Danny, who began doing his investigation of Hinton's paper trail. It turned out that his father and brother were both part of the scam and much of the thirty-five million pounds had been invested in property and spread among accounts that he controlled personally and others that he shared with his father and his brother. This was a right little rogue family business.

Quite a few million pounds were located in a variety of bank accounts and some cash had been invested in properties in Spain. We managed to track down a sizeable portion of the fraudulently obtained money and Helen set about going down the legal routes to impose sanctions to freeze all Hinton's assets. This would be quite a task. While she could start the process in the United Kingdom, she also had to work through the European legal processes as well and engage with the Spanish system in particular.

In the meantime, we were able to keep Tom Hinton close for a while and pretty much knew where he was at all times. We carried out his inquiries for him and fed him enough information to ensure that he was kept busy and would come back for more. Graham would meet up with him on a regular basis to brief him on the latest information we had gleaned and to encourage him to keep the investigation going. Helen managed to achieve a reasonable amount with her legal battles and froze a number of the Hinton family assets in the UK, Spain and Italy. At length, Hinton cut contact with Graham, vanished and we never heard from him again. I suspect he returned to Spain to try and move some more monies around as, even with some assets frozen, he was still a very wealthy man, with funds we didn't locate and those Helen could not get frozen by the courts.

Because of the success that we were having with tracing the financial trails of the fraudster, Helen recommended us to a number of other law firms. We began to receive a steady stream of instructions to locate funds that had effectively been stolen from various clients. Danny, in turn, was getting a lot of work from us at this time.

We carried out an investigation into a fraud in Norfolk, another property scam but one that was not anywhere near the scale of Hinton's. This time the police had actually got involved and this was quite remarkable for us because in general we found they would usually distance themselves from these kinds of investigations. In this case, we were able to give them a lot of information that they would not have otherwise received and they were very happy with our assistance.

We just hoped to help and we were trying to do what we thought was the right thing, trying to recover funds for people who had been the subject of fraud. And sometimes it worked and clients did indeed have their stolen funds returned. It would come as a great shock to all of us when, later on, we would be pursued ourselves by the law and charged with 'conspiracy to defraud by false representation'. This was down to Danny's efforts: he was getting information by blagging and it would be this that would be classed as false representation. In his work he pretended to be other people and, because we had given him the instructions for his work and paid him for it, the law decided this was a conspiracy. It was nonsense; it was clear that Danny got access to information in order to bring criminals to justice. We were not out to steal money. Our investigations centred on dubious and criminal practices and to get money back to people who had been the victims of crime. We were working for solicitors and barristers.

A number of the surveillance jobs that I worked on for both solicitors and private clients formed part of matrimonial investigations. One partner in these cases suspected their spouse of having an affair and they required evidence that could be provided in court during any subsequent divorce proceeding. I quite often employed a tracking device on the target vehicle in these jobs, but I always made sure that I got a letter of agreement from the client to cover myself. The use of a tracking device is only legal if you have the permission of the owner of the car and this would be permissible where the vehicle was in my client's name.

The tracker was encased in a heavy-duty plastic box and could be attached to a vehicle by very powerful magnets. The tracking unit itself, inside the box, was powered by a long-life battery pack that in real-world scenarios would generally last a good week or two. The signal it gave off could be broadcast using a normal mobile phone SIM card in the box. I had software that I could log into via my laptop and that meant I could happily sit in my car and follow the subject's vehicle at all times. If two people were on the task, one of us would tail the target while the other did the monitoring and would keep their partner updated with the location of the vehicle and its direction of travel. The tracker really was an excellent piece of equipment and came into its own on a number of occasions: it was highly accurate and it was possible to follow the signal from the SIM to within about five metres of the vehicle's location. It could also be set to trigger an alarm when the vehicle began moving. Invariably, I would install the tracker very late at night or early in the morning, usually placing it somewhere inside the rear bumper, where I had found the signal was the clearest. I would then return to my car to set up the software on my laptop to confirm I was receiving a signal. That was it; all done, then it was time to sit back and monitor the movements of the car.

Sometimes matrimonial investigations prompted strange reactions in the clients I worked with. I was tasked with putting a woman in Reading under surveillance by the solicitor representing her husband, who had an idea that she was seeing someone else but needed evidence of her adultery. He was going to Portugal to play golf with some friends for the weekend and she had told him that she would probably go to London with her sister, do a bit of shopping and see a West End show. They might even stay the night. This had got the husband still more suspicious.

I had managed to secure the tracker under the rear bumper of her Jeep Wrangler and watched as the husband drove away. I left the area and sat, out of sight, in my car waiting for the movement alarm to activate on the tracker. Nothing happened for a number of hours. I did the occasional drive past, just to make sure that her car was still on the drive, double-checking, even though I had a really good signal coming through from the SIM card. The husband rang from Heathrow to find out how things were going as he was waiting to board his plane and I was able to report that there had been no activity and that she was still at their property.

It wasn't until much later, around seven o'clock in the evening, that she finally drove away and I had no trouble in following her. She also ended up at Heathrow, but her destination was one of the airport hotels. She walked into the foyer and I had no doubt about where she was: the car was quite distinctive, bright-red, hard to miss really. I took some photographs of her leaving her vehicle with an overnight bag and followed her into the reception area and listened while she booked in. Now I knew what room she was using and I also knew what table number she had booked for dinner. I wandered into the restaurant, located the table and realised it was perfectly positioned for me to set up both my stills and video cameras to cover her.

She arrived at the table at just after half past eight, escorted by an unknown male companion. I started filming and was taking a few photos when her husband phoned. I quietly briefed him on the current situation with his wife and he asked for a detailed description of the male who was her dining companion. The husband believed he quite possibly knew who the bloke was from my description and asked if I could take a wander around the car park to try and locate a black Range Rover with private plates that would provide confirmation. This was a matter of a couple of minutes' work as the vehicle in question was coincidentally parked close to mine. The client was fine with my conclusion and said that I should stop my surveillance and go home. He asked me to restart the task back at their house the following afternoon, as she would probably stay out quite late. I mentioned the overnight bag, but the client did not seem too concerned. I headed home to run through my video coverage and still photos and typed up the day's report.

The following day, around ten in the morning, I checked the software on my laptop and the vehicle tracker confirmed that the target vehicle was still in the car park at the hotel. Pretty obviously she had stayed the night. I drove to the hotel just to make sure I had not been getting a false signal. After about ten minutes, purely by chance, the subject and the unknown male left the hotel, each heading to their own cars. I got the video up and running and filmed the subject as she put her bag in the car and then sat on the bonnet. The unknown male walked over from his car and positioned himself in front of her. They embraced tightly and she wrapped her legs around his back as they engaged in some very deep, hard kissing. It was all on video.

After they parted, I followed the subject back to her house. Around two hours later a car containing a female arrived and by the looks of her she was pretty obviously the subject's sister; they

144

looked like they could be twins. A taxi arrived at the house and took them, complete with overnight bags, to Reading railway station. I jumped on the same eastbound train to London and sat in the next carriage, where I could observe the pair without compromise. From Paddington mainline station I followed them onto the Underground and eventually they got out at Covent Garden, walked to the Waldorf hotel and into the foyer. I let them go at this stage and rang the client to report what was happening. He confirmed that the subject and the other woman were in fact twins and that he had spoken to her earlier in the day and everything that she said she was going to do had happened. They were staying at the Waldorf and they were going to get tickets for a show. I lifted off and made my way back to Reading to get my car and head home. I arranged to meet the client at his office the following week, where I would give him the full brief, the photographs and the videos I had taken.

The client turned out not to be in a place to accept the evidence before him. I passed him the incontrovertible story told in stills and video and handed him my typed report of the task. But as I briefed him on the meeting at the hotel with the unknown male he did not seem interested in what I had to tell him. He dismissed my report and made some garbled reference to knowing who the man was and confirming that he was close friends with his wife. Bloody right they were, I thought. He asked me for my invoice, wrote out a cheque there and then and that was the end of that. I headed back home. It was rather strange that I had got on the record everything that he required but he had somehow decided to blank out what was in plain sight in front of him. I never had any further contact from him.

Bob and I were tasked with a surveillance job in Manchester. He decided he was going to try and get his tracker onto the target's car, which proved to be a difficult task, as the vehicle was a bright-green TVR sports car and its rear bumper – and, indeed, most of the car – was constructed from fibreglass, giving little scope for attaching heavy-duty magnets. We had a go at about two o'clock in the morning, when Bob at last managed to secure the tracker to the engine block near the joint where the exhaust joined the engine. This was the only place he could find for a solid fix. I kept lookout up and down the road to make sure nobody spotted Bob. The plastic car was a fast motor but you wouldn't want to have to survive a crash in one.

The attachment worked and we carried out surveillance on the subject for about three days, joined by Mark, the motorbike operator. We started by sorting out our radio equipment together and doing voice procedure checks, before the TVR headed down the road. We managed to keep up until he reached a motorway and was gone in a flash. Not only could neither Bob nor I keep up with him but, had we been able to muster the sort of speed required, we would have been compromised straight away. Mark managed to stay with him but we told him to drop back as the tracker was working perfectly. We kept reporting the target's movements to Mark and eventually the car came to a halt just to the north of Huddersfield. Mark got to him a few minutes later and rang me with some bad news. The car was in a specialist tyre garage and had been mounted on an electronic ramp. The owner was underneath the car alongside the mechanic, both shining bright torches at the underside of the chassis. Would they spot the tracker box? This could be bad.

Bob and I parked nearby and we sat there wondering if the device would be compromised. The SIM card was untraceable and the tracker itself could not be traced either so that was not too bad in itself. The mild inconvenience would have been the fact they were reasonably expensive and it would be quite a wait to get a replacement as the bloke who got them for us was using a supplier in Germany. Our target would also probably be well and truly alerted to surveillance. The car was still up on the ramp and the fitter was messing about doing whatever while the target wandered around having a coffee and speaking on his mobile phone. Just in case he had called the police, we went to a café some distance away.

I had Bob's laptop and live-tracked the device. It remained at the garage for a while before the signal showed it was heading back to Manchester. We decided to let it run just in case the car owner or the mechanic had found it. The box was possibly on his passenger seat for all we knew. We drove slowly back to Manchester too and Mark did a ride past the target's house on his motorbike. He reported back that the car was on his driveway and the subject was nowhere to be seen; he was assumed to have gone inside his house. The tracker was very accurate when it had a good signal and, according to the software, it was exactly where the car was parked. I was relieved – he had not spotted it and possibly just mistook the black plastic box for part of the advanced design of the car.

The job was coming to an end and, later that night, again at about two in the morning, Bob and I wandered down the road to the subject's house. Bob got onto his back and manoeuvred himself under the engine, quite an achievement for a biggish bloke like him working in the restricted space under a sporty TVR. He managed to get hold of the tracker and wriggled himself back out while I kept watch for anyone taking a late walk.

We headed back to our hotel and had a few drinks in the room and chatted about how the whole episode had been a very close run thing.

THIRTEEN

I was fast asleep when I was rudely awoken by loud knocking and banging on my front door.

'Police, open the door!'

Bloody hell, what did they want at this time of night?

I dragged myself out of bed, threw on a bathrobe and opened the door. Two plainclothes policemen introduced themselves, showed their warrant cards and walked in. These were officers from the Met and SOCA (Serious Organised Crime Agency) and one of them told me of my right to remain silent. He was the inspector in charge of an inquiry in which, I now discovered, I was a feature.

I lived in a large farm complex outside Milton Keynes, one of four separate barn conversions, but the police thought I owned the lot and had sent a team of eighteen to get me. Bit of overkill! They really had not spent much time researching my circumstances – even a quick look at the electoral register would have revealed that I lived alone. I later discovered that they had knocked on my next-door neighbour's door first and the poor girl was scared half to death at the noise and shouting. All I could do was apologise to her. Realising the truth of the situation, the inspector sent all but four of his team away in their various minibuses.

I asked if it was all right to have a shower and a mug of coffee before I was taken away. After getting dressed I stepped out to have a cigarette and I was taken in an unmarked car to Milton Keynes police station where I was processed by the desk sergeant, had my photographs and fingerprints taken, DNA swab done, pockets emptied, shoelaces and belt removed and I was then put in a cell. Waiting in to be seen was one of the most mind-bogglingly, excruciatingly boring things I have ever experienced in my life and, yes, I did start counting the bricks. There was pretty much nothing else to do.

At long last they remembered me and I was escorted to an interview room, a plain room with a table, a twin-deck recording device and four chairs. I had asked for the duty solicitor to be present and we had to wait for him before the questioning could start. I was able to have a quick chat with him beforehand – he had been briefed by the officers about their inquiry and he suggested that I responded 'No comment' throughout the interview or even remain totally silent.

I had been brought in for questioning about a charge of conspiracy to defraud, as I mentioned in the previous chapter. The problems were in our investigation methods – we would sometimes gain sensitive information on individuals and companies and now this was going to cause me a great deal of trouble.

I took the solicitor's advice and replied to each question with a resolute, 'No comment.' I could tell that they were not impressed – not surprisingly, the police do like to get people under arrest to actually enter into some kind of dialogue with them. In all, I did the no-commenting for eight hours solid, which was very laborious, but if nothing else the line of questioning gave me and the solicitor a good idea of where they were going with the investigation and how much real information they had gathered on the case at this early stage. I was bailed to be interviewed again in one month, the venue to be Kingston police station near the Thames. This was some seventy miles away to the south-west of London and quite a distance to travel.

As we were leaving the building I asked if I could have a lift back to the farm but was told that I would have to get a taxi back. The search team would be there to hand over my keys as they were on the verge of finishing up rummaging around. I got back to find that my computer was still at home, along with my mobile phone but my laptop was gone. Apparently they had been unable to make an image of the hard drive, as they had done with my desktop. They left a couple of sheets of receipts detailing everything that they had removed which I had to read and sign, while the commander countersigned everything. It would be a few years before I would see my possessions again and then only after I bothered them constantly with requests. Even my local MP got involved and badgered them too.

The mobile phone bothered me. I was very wary of the police allowing me to keep hold of it and I wondered what they might have installed on it or how they might track it. For security's sake, I removed the battery and the SIM card and went into town to get a new mobile phone with a different number. I didn't trust the police and I was certainly not going to start trusting SOCA.

Graham rang me to say that he was in Spain and that some Met and/or SOCA representative had rung him and asked him to return to the UK to be interviewed under caution. Graham told him that they would have to wait until he was coming over; he did not intend to just turn up at their behest, but – unlike me – he had not been arrested. The Met were going charge me with hacking offences and it was in connection with this that they wanted to interview Graham. He had also had his property in Hertfordshire turned over at the same time as I was being raided. At least – his former house. He and his family had since moved to Spain and the couple who now lived in that property had shown their passports to prove that not only were neither of them Graham but they were in fact US citizens. When I heard this story, I hoped that they would put a complaint in about this treatment. I heard later that the SOCA people had been heavy-handed with the man as he was protesting his innocence.

I had my second round of questioning at Kingston, which again went on for a good few hours. At length, I was offered a break and told the interviewing officer that I would not mind having a smoke. They allowed me to go into the courtyard at the back of the station, escorted by a different officer, who was also a smoker and, it turned out, glad of the chance to join me. He spoke with a Northern Irish accent and, when we were outside, he tipped me off. I was also going to be charged for illegal possession of ammunition, he revealed, and I should think of a reason for the police's discovery of some old ammunition in my garage. I thought this officer's kindness was an unusual gesture and it did cross my mind that he might have been in the RUC prior to transferring to the Met. It wouldn't be that unusual a career path to take.

I had decided to speak out during this latest interview, instead of simply remaining in 'no comment' mode. I had a reasonable excuse for possessing three rounds of Browning 9mm ammunition and hoped that eventually this charge would be dropped. I told the officers that I had not had a look at the contents of what was a box within a box at the very back of my garage for about twenty years. I was totally unaware that those rounds were there. I explained that I had been an undercover soldier for years and had had thousands of rounds of ammunition at my disposal at various times. I told them about the time I rung the police armed response team in the local city area, having been given the name of the team leader by an old SAS mate of mine. He was retained as their specialist driving instructor. At that time I had realised that I possessed a box of two hundred rounds of ammunition and a flash-bang grenade. I asked if I could dispose of them safely and he agreed. I put the ammo in a plastic bag, went to the police firearms range and handed them over to this contact at a side gate. I had followed his instructions to the letter. So, I asked now, why on earth would I want to keep three rounds of twenty-five-year-old ammunition back? It did not make sense. They listened intently but seemed quite uninterested in my story; the charge was there to stay.

It was not only Graham and I who were in trouble. Danny and two other people he had sub-contracted were also arrested. Danny had sold his old laptop some months beforehand; he had put it up for sale for a couple of hundred pounds on some internet site. He had rather foolishly only wiped the hard drive rather than doing the sensible thing and destroying it entirely. The cash buyer had turned out to be a SOCA officer claiming to have seen his online advert. I could not help thinking that there was some kind of illegal subterfuge carried out by SOCA. How had they found out about the sale of the old laptop?

We were all charged by SOCA with conspiracy to defraud by false representation. We were to appear at Kingston magistrates court to make our pleas. SOCA asked for us to be held on remand to await trials but, noting that we had attended interviews as required, the magistrate granted bail before our Crown Court trial, set for a few weeks' time in Kingston.

My solicitor asked for two character references, preferably from prominent members of society. I think he was very surprised to hear that I was pretty sure I could get one off a peer of the realm and was certain to be able to get the other from a retired colonel. My friendship with the lord in question dated back to my time in Northern Ireland with the FRU, when I lived in his massive, six-bedroom hunting lodge on a lovely country estate. He had a river running through the grounds and I was allowed to fish both banks along the whole stretch that was on his property: it was brilliant. I knew him reasonably well and he was quite aware of my background and what I did for the army; he had been an officer in a cavalry regiment before retiring to run the family estate and he was also a senior member of the Ulster Defence Regiment. The colonel had been my commanding officer when I served in the Royal Armoured Corps. I was his driver and he had promoted me twice. He was also a country sports fanatic and excelled at fly-fishing and deer-stalking. We would chat away about both pastimes and he was well aware of my passion for angling.

Both men came through with excellent references. The lord mentioned that soldiers who worked at the FRU were specially selected to be of good character and he was aware that I would have been vetted quite intensely for that role. I was given access to secret documents and information on a daily basis and from time to time I would have been in contact with top-secret operational matters. My old commanding officer gave me an equally gleaming write-up, mentioning that he had chosen me to be his driver because of the promise I had shown as a soldier. He said I was always smart and good at my job. As his driver I had shown exceptional qualities and was always professional in my daily routine. He had supported my application for special duties as he considered that I had all the right qualities to pass selection and work in that position. He found me to be amusing, likeable, well-read and honest and he mentioned that we had shared interests in rugby and fly-fishing and that I demonstrated an above-average ability to apply my military skills and commanded respect. He considered me to be a natural leader and he never found me wanting when I was working under pressure with responsibility. He made a note of my wry sense of humour, on display however tough things were. I was sure these glowing references would definitely have some kind of influence on the judge.

Eventually, the date arrived to appear at Kingston Crown Court. This was now a serious business and five of us sat behind a glass panel being watched by press and members of the public. I knew that the crimes we were being charged with did not make us a threat to the public and I felt reasonably sure that we would be given suspended sentences. One of my co-defendants faced only one count – and even that was a bit flimsy. His barrister was absolutely superb and convinced the judge that the charge should be dropped and his offence was actually a breach of data protection. He was not part of the conspiracy that touched the rest of us. He was duly released and had soon departed with his solicitor and barrister. I was there on eight counts, John and Graham were up on six counts each and Danny faced charges on all counts.

Graham was to face an extra charge after we walked out of the court hearing one lunchtime and I spotted the police inspector from the Met who had arrested me on computer hacking charges. No sooner had I mentioned it to Graham when they approached us and asked him to go to a side room. He was arrested too.

One of the nuisance factors of being in court was the press, who became a constant source of irritation. One hack in particular was approaching me all the time when we had breaks outside the hearing. He even came up to me when I was in discussions with my barrister who at one stage told him to 'Fuck off'. My barrister was a steely-eyed Glaswegian who had been in the Parachute Regiment and the SAS before studying law and, despite his change of profession, he had an air about him that made you think that he might just rip your head off if things went badly. The hack shrugged his shoulders and walked away.

There was something about this particular reporter that rung a bell – he worked for the *Guardian* and he seemed vaguely familiar but I could not quite pull his identity out of my memory bank. When I got home that evening, I went through my old invoices and reports and I trawled my emails, looking for any mention of this man. Eventually, I found exactly what I was looking for. About six or seven years previously I had been introduced to this journalist by a mutual acquaintance in London. He wanted some personal information about an MP, very personal details that included his mobile phone records and banking history over a certain period. I managed to get that information and now I even found a copy of the remittance note from the *Guardian*; I had been paid just over three thousand pounds for the information. Another invoice and remittance for two hundred and fifty pounds followed about two weeks later and I had that too. His name was on the authority to release the funds. I also found my bank statements for those weeks showing the transfers and I printed them off.

The following day I had a quick chat with my solicitor before going into court. He was aware that this journalist was becoming a total pest and I showed him the paperwork. He put the paperwork into his folder with a big laugh. Right on cue, the reporter made his first unwelcome appearance of the day. I gave him a look and announced, 'You don't remember me, do you?' He looked at me quizzically and I prompted him by mentioning the name of our mutual friend who had introduced us many years beforehand. He still did not seem to click. I proceeded to remind him about the work that I had carried out for him and also told him that my solicitor had copies of all the relevant paperwork and that if he did not back off and leave me alone then we would see to it that SOCA and the Met would be receiving copies. He could well find that he would become part of the case that he was reporting on. He backed off and I did not get much hassle from him after that.

As the case progressed it was becoming quite evident that the judge had already found us guilty. My optimism about how the charges were likely to be seen now seemed badly misguided and as for the first-class references from the lord and the colonel, the court might as well have shredded them. After the fifth co-defendant had his case thrown out, the remaining barristers also had asked that our charges were downgraded from conspiracy to data protection breaches, as we could have proved that, as investigators, we had the right to carry out our enquiries. The judge was having none of it and the charges were to remain the same.

Graham's barrister caught out one of the SOCA officers in cross-examination. The officer admitted that not all of the evidence had been submitted to both the prosecution and the defence. A key bedrock of British court law had been ignored;

he was admitting that he had given the prosecution an advantage in their case. The barrister immediately looked to the judge and asked that the jury be removed from the court. In fluent legal jargon he asked that the case be dismissed. By way of response, the judge asked the SOCA officer where the paperwork was and the court eventually ascertained that it was in Manchester, where SOCA had its headquarters. It was a fiasco, what we came to know as the 'Manchester file'.

The Manchester file was duly sent for and I remember my solicitor saying that he thought the file would either be lost or destroyed that very night. He had always believed that we were not the real target for SOCA. He said that the agency had wasted a great deal of money on another case and we were linked in some way to this other case. They just had to be seen to get convictions. We were the fall guys for their botched enquiry. They had obviously got loads of damning information on us from Danny's poorly erased laptop, as well, which did not help matters.

As the solicitor predicted, the Manchester file never appeared and other SOCA paperwork proved to be equally questionable: they had not declared how their investigation had begun and would not discuss where the charges originated. Surely, a dodgy bit of detective work had gone on somewhere here? We felt it was very likely that they had probably broken the law to get what they did on us. The barrister asked the judge again to dismiss the charges and throw the case out but he would not do it. Instead, he said that the case would be adjourned for a month to allow the SOCA team to get their house in order and to cross the Ts and dot the Is. It would appear that the judge was able to dismiss a point of law and carry on as he deemed fit. I said to my barrister that I thought I should plead guilty right now. I knew that if I was to make the plea early, the sentence would be shorter and, as I already was sure the judge was going to instruct the jury to find us guilty, now was the time to do it. She agreed. At least with the court adjournment over December I would get to spend Christmas with my family and friends which was a bonus.

I then had to return to court to be sentenced for possession of ammunition – they had also kept this charge. I was sentenced to four months' imprisonment which, thankfully, was to run concurrently with the sentence I would be receiving for the other conspiracy charges. I had originally been arrested on suspicion of offences that came under the Data Protection Act, which would have been defendable as a private investigator. The information we had gathered was necessary for the purposes of preventing or detecting crime. My barrister also mentioned that, in our particular circumstances, the information was justified as being in the public interest. He also argued that, because I did not know how Danny got his information, I could not possibly be part of a conspiracy. Further, I was acting in a role in pursuing inquiries on behalf of corporate and professional clients and the prevention of further crimes was certainly in the public interest.

My barrister also tried to instigate an abuse of process in the trial because the original charge had been ramped up to an offence under the Criminal Law Act over a year after the original arrest. This had been done when I returned to answer bail conditions at Staines police station. He claimed this was unjust and unfair and that any paperwork that had passed between SOCA, the CPS and the data protection commissioner must be made available to the defence team. Our requests to be tried under the lesser charge were turned down on all counts, just as application for the missing files came to nothing.

The first charge I faced concerned an inquiry on behalf of a marketing services company who were contemplating legal proceedings against an individual. They had been duped into giving a sub-contractor fourteen thousand pounds. He did not carry out the work but kept the money, defaulting on his contractual agreement. He had been paid in advance and, using Danny to do the research, I was able to locate the money. Secondly, I was charged with investigating a company director who was suspected of receiving third-party payments from a competitor in exchange for information about his own company contracts and clients. I was able to identify the third party, how much contact they had and how much money he had been paid.

There was more: I was able to provide information to a foreign exchange business that had lost money to a company that was basically set up to steal deposits made on off-plan sales of Spanish properties that did not even exist. This ran into several hundreds of thousands of pounds and we had given some of this information quite freely to Norfolk police officers who were also investigating the same fraudsters. I had also carried out an investigation into an individual who had been given forty thousand pounds as part of a business venture. He had denied that he had received the funds and we were able to investigate and prove where the money had been hidden.

Further, I had carried out some research on behalf of another private investigator into a mortgage fraud scam being carried out in the Midlands. I was able to provide him with information that showed how the individual was carrying out the mortgage frauds and how much he had stolen. I felt this was yet another good, public-interest investigation – yet it was also included in my charge list. There were two other, similar investigations, carried out against fraudsters on behalf of solicitors for their clients.

I was found guilty on all counts. In the eyes of the law, I had broken the law by investigating and finding fraud and proving thefts. 'The law is an ass,' that famous saying attributed to Charles Dickens, seemed entirely appropriate on that day.

All the barristers came to the same conclusion and all defendants pleaded guilty, a sentencing date was set and we all went home. I was still convinced that we would get suspended sentences. Yet when we returned and lined up to face the judge, I was sentenced to eight months' imprisonment and my heart sank as the word 'suspended' did not follow. We were led away from the box through a door at the back of the room and taken to a dispersal area under the courtroom. We were all handcuffed to guards from Group 4 security as we were led away. I was horrified to hear that we were going to be taken to Wandsworth prison. It had a grim reputation and I just could not believe what was happening. I was totally confused and even at this late stage I kept thinking that, at any moment, I was going to be led back into the courtroom and have the judge tell me he had done this to teach me a lesson and he was now going to release me under caution. Unfortunately, I was kidding myself and along with my three colleagues I was ordered into a hard seat in the cramped prison transport. Before we were led out of the holding area, we were stripped of our belts and shoelaces just as I had been when I was first arrested.

Ironically, Graham and I still faced computer-hacking charges and we were not supposed to have any contact with each other. Of course, not only had we just been sentenced together, but we would likely be in contact with each other every day. Indeed, it would turn out we were to actually share the same cell. By that point I was only surprised they did not try and bring charges against us for being in breach of bail conditions: it felt like just the kind of thing that the courts would be capable of doing.

I had left my car and mobile with Nikki and Simon, the colleagues from my *Penthouse* days. They lived nearby and I had been staying with them to save on travel time and petrol money going back and forth from Milton Keynes to Kingston. They were very helpful and we still remain great friends. I had already sent an email to my brother asking him to let certain people know the outcome if it went the wrong way – mostly my immediate family and very close friends. If he heard from me in person then everything was fine and that meant I had walked from the court. If he heard from Nikki or Simon then I had pretty obviously been sent down. The email contained my partner's phone details, and also my ex-wife's, my daughters' and, of course, my parents, who were blissfully unaware of all of this. Nikki and Simon set about the task of letting my brother know what had gone on in court. I had not told anyone about the court cases as I had totally convinced myself that I would get a suspended sentence and I knew it would stop them from worrying if they were kept in the dark. My father agreed with my brother that he would cover the rental payments on my place at the farm while I was away, bless him. It was nice to have a dad who would bail me out from time to time. My landlord, Rob, was an understanding bloke and my brother kept in touch to assure him that the rent would be covered.

My ex-wife inadvertently panicked my youngest daughter when she heard the news. My daughter saw her go into whispered conversations with people on the phone in a different room, trying to keep my sentence secret. My poor daughter thought that I had died and that my passing was being kept from her. She later revealed that, given the options, she was actually really relieved that I had 'only' been sent to prison. She had a good head on her shoulders and after my release I took her to the prison and pointed out the various wings where I had been and described the routine of my life in there. I think she found it very useful to have some closure. I was glad I did it.

FOURTEEN

I looked out of the tinted window of the prison van and saw two blokes and a girl on a grassy patch in a south London park. They were scruffily dressed and held up cans of beer in a mock salute directed my way.

The next sight was not so amusing and my heart sank: the daunting vision of the front gates of Wandsworth prison rose up before me. I had seen some ghastly things in my life but this beat them all hands down.

My right wrist was handcuffed to a recess in the hard plastic seat and I was further caged in a cubicle in which I could barely get my legs straight, never mind stretch them out. The prison gates opened and closed behind us. One by one we were released from our restrictive booths and told to follow the leading prison officer, each of us escorted by two other guards. I felt numb. I felt uneasy. This was totally out of my comfort zone and even though I had been through tough interrogation scenarios along with escape and evasion exercises during my selection for special duties, nothing prepared me for this moment.

We joined a queue of other new inmates until eventually we reached a waiting room, where we were told to sit down. Graham and I sat together and just nervously looked at each other and shook our heads in disbelief: this was about as bad as it got. We were called forward and searched, told to sit in a large wooden chair which apparently detected the presence of drugs and then were led into a room and interviewed by a nurse. A quick medical questionnaire was filled in and we were told to strip to our underwear and hand in all our clothes and possessions. The only thing I was allowed to keep were my shoes, with the laces removed. In this rather undignified condition we were led to the main part of the prison, clad in a baggy grey tracksuit and carrying bedding and a towel. It looked all the more ridiculous as we were all wearing smart, black leather shoes as we had gone to court wearing suits. If it was not so pathetic and serious it could have almost been comedic.

Wandsworth prison was built in the early 1850s and houses around eighteen hundred inmates. It is an austere, menacing institution and the walk along the landing was a fraught experience. The established prisoners banged the doors and yelled obscenities as the new kids took up their residences. Luckily, Graham and I were put in the same cell to our great relief. Our new home was furnished with a metal-framed bunk bed and plastic-coated mattresses, two plastic chairs and a table with a television on top. There was a small handbasin and an open, metal-rimmed toilet. We both agreed immediately that this would only be used for urinating and that other ablutions could wait until we were allowed into the communal shower and toilet area. It would have been inhumane to have had to have put up with something so personal in such close proximity.

About an hour later, the prison officers arrived on the landing, opening the cell doors. The moment of truth had arrived and we very quietly and nervously emerged from our cell. We were greeted by other prisoners, everyone shook hands and there were lots of questions about what we were in for, the length of our sentences and so on. The tirade of abuse that we had endured while walking to the cells had just been a sick initiation that every new prisoner had to go through. It was a kind of tribal reception and in person the other prisoners were not so terrifying.

Bargaining immediately began. Chocolate and 'burn' (tobacco) were sought-after commodities. All prisoners who smoked were given one pack of Gold Leaf when they arrived, along with Rizla papers and a disposable lighter. Those who did not smoke were given a few small bars of chocolate. 'Got any burn, mate?' was soon the most-used phrase I had ever heard in my entire life.

Existence inside Wandsworth was tedious, to say the least. Meals were collected by floor, one level going at a time, prisoners taking their food back to the cells. The cell doors were locked most of the time, apart from an hour or so during the day in which inmates would shower, do laundry, get to the phone or just stand around outside the cells discussing criminal activities with their colleagues. Getting outside to wander in the fresh air was a rare event and even when we did get out of the building, most inmates would amble around the yard discussing crimes they had already committed and planning others for the future. Yard time was so restricted due to a shortage of prison officers and because of health and safety legislation. All of us were pretty much locked away inside our cells for some twenty-three hours a day. It was not a good place to be and the prison officers were so irritatingly ignorant that the place was always on a knife edge. Fights, arguments and room-smashing were regular occurrences.

Graham and I both kept ourselves to ourselves and, luckily, because we were both quite intelligent blokes, passed the time with reasonable conversation. Both of us had links to the military and it was during one of these chats, when I was telling him about some of the operations I had been involved in, that he said I was 'like no other soldier' he had ever met. The only bone of contention between us was the television. The usual debate revolved around football which I detested and Graham loved. But, apart from the inevitable *Match of the Day* debate, everything else was pretty much hunky-dory.

On our first morning a prison officer arrived with a clipboard and announced, 'Mr Lewis, downstairs for meds.'

I looked at him in an inquiring way and questioned, 'Meds?'

He repeated that I was to go down to the main hall and join the queue for medication and, rather bemused, I wandered down to the stairs. I was confronted by a pretty shocking scene: in prison, all the drug-abusers are given methadone to help control their problem and the queue was filled with what looked like the walking dead; hunched over, grey-faced, shaking, skinny blokes. I spoke to the nurse who was handing the medicines out and she cleared up my presence. Apparently, when I filled in the lifestyle questionnaire she had decided that my age and my drinking and eating routine meant I needed some kind of vitamin and mineral substitute. I was able to convince her that I really didn't need anything, was taken off the list and I returned to my cell. I had to do it all over again the next day. The prison service is administratively incompetent and for the next four mornings I had to explain to the officer that I had been taken off the 'meds' list until, eventually, the early morning calls stopped.

Life was so monotonous and every day dragged until one morning a slip of paper slid under the door: I had a visitor at two o'clock that day. No other information was forthcoming and I was intrigued to find out who applied for and got permission to visit. I entered the visitor's hall – after being searched twice en route – and saw the big, beaming smile of my mate Bob. In front of him on the table were two large cups of coffee, three chocolate muffins, four bars of chocolate and a big slice of lemon drizzle cake. He pointed at the feast and told me to get stuck in, it was all for me. Bob was my absolute rock throughout this period; he kept my partner up to speed with what was going on, he rang my brother to let him have any updates for the rest of my family and friends. He was just such a star; I cannot thank him enough for his friendship.

I was only in Wandsworth for a couple of weeks before I was moved. As ever, there was no warning of what was to happen. The cell door opened one morning and an officer said, 'Mr Lewis, grab your stuff and follow me, you are going to C wing.'

The guard said I was being transferred the following morning to HMP Hewell. I'd never heard of the place. Graham was staying and we simply shook hands, said our farewells and off I went, to be put in a cell with a young lad called Zak. He was a hilarious guy and as soon as the door had shut he asked me if I wanted to use the phone, I looked at him quizzically, but he wasn't making it up. He had three mobile phones secreted around the cell. One was inside the metal tubing of the bed frame, another lay inside a mattress and the other was stashed behind some old water pipes. He had rigged up an ingenious little charger pack using some batteries, masking tape and two strands of copper.

I politely declined as mobile usage was forbidden and if I were to be caught I would take an automatic trip to the segregation unit and have a month added to my sentence. It was quite ironic, really, as most of the mobile phones in prison were brought in and sold to the inmates by the prison officers. They followed a routine of giving those who wanted a phone the details of their wife's or girlfriend's bank and this would be passed to a family member and the account would be credited with the arranged amount. The officers in on the scheme were charging two hundred pounds for which they provided a ten-pound supermarket mobile phone – it was a nice little earner. During my one night sharing with Zak he told me how to get hold not only of phones but also alcohol and marijuana; he was an absolute mine of prison information. I did not have any requirement for what he was describing but it was amusing to listen to him. He also told me that HMP Hewell was near Redditch and that it had an open wing for prisoners who posed no threat or had served a decent amount of their sentence. I imagined I would probably be going there. As the old saying goes, 'Never assume the obvious.'

I arrived at Hewell in the same kind of transport as delivered me to Wandsworth – shackled to a hard plastic seat and no room at all to stretch my legs. There were three other prisoners transferred along with me and we picked up another two from

Winson Green prison, Birmingham, on our journey. On arrival a few hours later, I had to go through the usual inward routine with the prison officers and the nurse until, eventually, I was led onto B wing and shown to my cell. It was hardly an open wing and I asked the prison officer if I was just staying there until I was to be taken to the open side. She said I was going to be staying put. My sentence was not long enough to allow me to transition to an open wing. I was living alongside murderers, armed robbers and drug dealers. A sobering thought indeed. When I walked along the ground floor the other inmates on the wing were on recreation and I did not get the door banging and yelling welcome, although those who were there did stare at me. Within less than a minute there was a lad at my door, 'Got any burn, mate?' Bloody hell, does it never stop? I thought.

I was in a cell by myself until the door opened later that evening and in walked my new cellmate, Shane. He was from Coventry and had been sentenced to seven years for arson. We shook hands and did the small talk and the inevitable question of tobacco raised its head. As he was going to be my cellmate and assured me that he had some burn ordered in the canteen the next day I told him where I hid my stash. He thanked me and proceeded to pull out five lighters from various pockets – my new arsonist mate had a collection of disposable incendiary devices on him: hilarious.

We got deeper into conversation and he revealed he had been living in a flat and had been having an argument with his landlord about the rent being raised. He couldn't afford the new amount and, in retribution for having to leave, he had set fire to the place. He also sent a text message to his landlord, admitting what he had done. He was, of course, arrested an hour later. There had been occupied flats both above and below his and his severe sentence reflected the danger he'd caused.

This was Shane's third time in HMP Hewell – his previous sentences had been served for fighting and car theft – he knew one or two other prisoners on the wing and knew two of the prison officers. Most of the other inmates were from the Birmingham and Coventry areas and there was a very high percentage of Albanians, Serbs and Croats, mostly inside for credit card theft, fraud and card cloning. The majority of them could not read or write and spoke a rough sort of pidgin English. I was soon able to turn this to my advantage.

While Shane and I were chatting one day the mail arrived; two letters for me and one for him. He just stared at his. When he at last opened it, he asked if I could read it as he could not, and nor could he write. I went through the letter for him and he asked if he could dictate a reply, which I wrote up. It also came to light that the lad in the cell next to ours could not write but he at least could read a little, with some difficulty. I became secretary to both of them. Word spread to the Eastern European crowd that I could fill in forms. The prison regime lived on forms – there was an application to be completed for just about anything and everything, but prison officers were resolute in not assisting anyone in coping with their own mania for paperwork. Anybody who approached an officer asking for help, explaining they couldn't read or write would usually be dismissed with a 'Tough shit.' Suddenly, I had a daily queue at recreation time, which turned into a right little business. For every form I filled in or letter I read there was a gift – usually sugar, coffee, teabags and the occasional cigarette offered up as well. My shelves piled up with what, believe me, were all genuine luxuries for those of us inside.

One evening the alarms suddenly began screeching on our wing, indicating a disturbance. One of the druggies had got into an altercation with the prison officer escorting him back from collecting his methadone. The conflict escalated into a full-scale fight as prison officers ran to the wing from all directions. The inmate took a beating from six officers until, eventually, they manhandled him into his cell. He wasn't done yet, going on to smash his television against the door and slamming a heavy plastic chair against the walls and his door.

He was howling like a dog. Throughout this I was lying on the top bunk in my cell, watching *Mastermind*, while Shane was hanging out of the window as best he could, smoking some weed. It didn't seem to be a major incident, until the whole wing went haywire, everybody following the lead of the cell-smasher. I could hear shouts and screams and the smashing of objects from all over the wing; it was crazy. Shane looked at me and suggested we should trash our cell, too. I glared at him and said, 'Mate, I'm watching *Mastermind* and I'm telling you now we are not wrecking the cell.' He looked at me, shrugged his shoulders and rather begrudgingly agreed. He went back to smoking his weed. No wonder he was in and out of prison all the time.

One of the female officers came to our cell two days later and asked if we wanted to move to the top floor. A much bigger cell had become vacant, boasting two single beds, a proper toilet in a separate area with a door and a view out of the window that faced a forest and open countryside. We snapped it up and, as we wandered along the third floor, I looked at Shane and said, 'We've got this because we didn't smash our cell, mate.' He agreed that I was probably right.

There were some real characters in Hewell. I was chatting to one of the older blokes, well into his late sixties, when he let slip that he was also an ex-soldier. His nickname was 'Pops' and he had been in the Coldstream Guards; further chat revealed that he was in for murder. He explained that he had found out that a drug dealer was trying to get his teenage daughter to buy crack cocaine and had gone around to the dealer's house and caved his head in with a hammer. He did not seem the slightest bit bothered about his actions and I suppose there would be plenty of us who would feel a certain empathy. I had a young daughter myself and it would be foolish of me to think that I would never do the same under those circumstances. Pops worked in the prison officer's station, doing general cleaning, filling the water boiler, making coffee and sweeping up but he was fed up with it and wanted to hand the job over to someone else. I had been doing an OCR course to obtain a vocational qualification in computing at the education wing and had just finished, passing the subject. I was keen to do something else. During recreation Pops and I wandered down to the screw's office and asked if I could take over his role. The guards had their usual reaction – not caring at all one way or another and so I started the next day. Shane and I enjoyed the perks of the job, including getting a load of extra sugar, teabags and coffee, along with the luxury of sharing in the prison officers' chocolate biscuits from time to time.

Irritatingly for the screws, any time they wanted something doing in the office, one of them had to walk up three flights of stairs, along the corridor and let me out of my cell at the end of the landing. When I finished the job, a screw would then have to return with me to lock me back in again. I came up with a plan. I approached the wing governor in the office and outlined the routine and why it was so tiresome. He nodded at me to continue. 'So, why don't you give me my own cell key?' I asked. If they wanted me down in the office, I said, they could just announce my name on the prison PA system and I would let myself out and lock the door behind me.

The wing governor stared at me, a big grin on his face, and simply said, 'OK. I'll get a key for you.' That was it, I had my very own cell key. I could not believe he had given it to me; it was hilarious.

One day, when I had just got back to my cell after recreation, Shane wandered into the room with one of the lads from the cell next door. They had been tipped off that he was going to have his cell searched in an hour or so and he was asking Shane to hold his weed until after the search was over. Shane looked at me and I just shook my head and told him it was nothing to do with me. I did not even smoke the stuff. But the lad from next door had promised Shane a share in his contraband if he did hide it and this was too good an offer for Shane to turn down.

The two lads in the cell next door were both inside for armed robbery. They had robbed a supermarket in Coventry and got into a tussle with the owner, who was in no mood to give up easily. He would not let them near the cash till and continued to fight them off even though they were armed. One of the young men leapt over the counter and, as he did, his T-shirt rode up and displayed his name conveniently tattooed across his lower back. All was revealed to the police in blazing technicolour when they took a look at the CCTV coverage. The two of them were arrested within the hour and were now doing nine years. In the end, the cell search did not take place, but Shane made sure he still received his share of weed for providing the service.

'The governor wants to see you.'

There were two prison officers at my cell door. They were there to escort me to another wing, where I was greeted by another two uniformed officers and a man dressed in a suit and tie sitting behind a desk in a pretty stark administrative office. He was the governor of the prison and I stood about six feet away from him with four prison officers in close proximity. It really was like a scene from the 1970s film *Scum* – that violent and controversial film about life in a youth detention centre.

I had been writing to various people to try and secure my release but there was a problem in getting me out because of the firearms offence. I had been sentenced to eight months, automatically reduced to four months of served time, and the system allowed another halving of this period for good behaviour as long as I was using an electronic tagging system. I had applied for the second reduction but had been automatically denied because of the three bullets. I was livid and had written to all the people I could think of to assist in getting out at the two-month point, including my old commanding officer and my local MP, one-time Conservative leadership candidate Andrea Leadsom. Both had written compelling letters on my behalf but the governor wanted to interview me himself.

As we talked, he mentioned that he had also been in the army and, coincidentally, he had served in Hohne, Germany and at one of the garrisons in Cyprus at the same time as I had. We calculated that we might well have played rugby against each other for our respective regiments. This at least established some common ground, and I made my case for early release all the more confidently. He assured me that he would give my request plenty of thought and let me know. I was returned to my wing, where I told the officers escorting me that I could let myself back in now as I had my key. Both looked at me in a bit of an odd way and insisted on taking me to my cell and locking me back inside.

The key continued to come in handy. I was watching the television one evening with Shane and asked if he fancied a sandwich. He looked at me as if I had two heads – you couldn't just go down to the kitchen any time you fancied. Well, I had a key, so I could. I let myself out of the cell and wandered down to the kitchen; nobody about. I was buttering some bread slices when the governor walked through on his evening rounds. I panicked and was convinced I was going to be seriously in the shit. He looked at me in surprise. 'Mr Lewis, exactly what are you doing?' I said I was making a ham sandwich and asked if he wanted one as well. He grinned and said, 'Yes, go on, then.'

I had got away with it.

I returned to my cell and mentioned my encounter to Shane who was amazed that the governor had not got me banged up in the segregation unit for my little culinary meander.

The following morning the cell door opened and the governor, accompanied by his usual phalanx of four officers, entered. Initially, I thought I was about to get a cell search, but the governor handed over a clipboard and a pen.

I started to read the forms on the board carefully.

'I suggest you just sign, Mr Lewis,' he said, clearly not used to hanging around.

I had read enough to see that this was the agreement for my early release. He had authorised the electronic tag and I was to be released the following morning; I was over the moon.

I needed to do a bit of organising first as, while I had been away, my friends Nikki and Simon had been looking after my car and my mobile phone. They agreed to pick me up from Redditch. My visitors at Hewell had included my brother, a few old army mates and my partner. I was glad that they would no longer need to make that awful trip. Bob, the guy who had come to see me at Wandsworth, had been a regular too and, between them, they had kept everyone informed of what was going on. None of them knew this was about to happen though.

I worked my way through the release process and was given my suit and shirt back. It felt strange to be wearing normal clothes instead of the prison tracksuit and slip-on shoes. I even had my laces, tie and belt. I was given my cigarettes, lighter and wallet and, strangely enough, had some cash to cover my transport back home. I was also given the funds that remained in my canteen account. I headed to the release area and could see my two friends and my car. It felt odd.

'Mr Lewis ... don't let me see you again, please.' This was one of the female prison officers on our wing. She was actually one of the few competent officers I had encountered, and I readily promised her that I did not intend to be seen inside again. With that, I walked out of the gates.

I met my friends and had my first normal cigarette in two months. I decided that I wanted to drive myself and we headed out towards the M40 motorway, having made a brief stop at the main gate to have a photograph taken outside the prison. I don't know why we did that – maybe it was something to show my grandchildren in years to come. I had been in prison for just a few weeks, but the feeling of euphoria on my release was quite amazing. I also had slight anxiety and experienced what I assume was agoraphobia. It seemed quite a strong reaction after only eight weeks inside. I thought about people who spend eight years in prison. What must they go through when they are at last released? They must experience outrageous emotions and maybe that was why a lot ended up going back. I know it is a cliché, but I completely understood how it would be easy to get institutionalised.

I dropped my friends off and headed home. This still felt so strange and in a way quite scary. I was desperate to speak to my partner and my daughters, but she was in work and my youngest was in school. I spoke to my eldest daughter; things were fine, she said, and she joked, 'It's time you grew up.'

I had to spend some time on my own back home at my converted barn in Northamptonshire. My partner was living in Yorkshire and would head down at the weekend. I invited Bob and his partner up on the Saturday and we intended to spend the whole day in the pub. It turned out to be a gorgeous day and we sat outside in the beer garden, soaking up the sun, just eating, drinking and laughing.

The only dampener on my mood was the knowledge that I had to be back home and indoors by seven o'clock for the curfew that ran overnight until seven in the morning. It was a bit of a pain but certainly far better than the alternative. I had been fitted with an electronic tag around my ankle, what Bob referred to as my 'Peckham Rolex'. I had to stay within the confines of the barn building and staff in the monitoring station would be able to tell if I tried to sneak out – or so they claimed.

I put this to the test on another beautiful evening, when my neighbours at the farm complex were outside in the courtyard area having a barbeque and drinks. I stood in my doorway chatting – they all knew my circumstances. I decided to chance my arm and join them outside. I moved out of the building and then rang the monitoring station to say that I wanted to sit outside on the patio area to make the most of the sunny weather. I didn't let on that I was already just outside my four walls. The operator told me this would be impossible and that I had to remain indoors otherwise I would be picked up and returned to prison. He said that he was looking at my signal and that he knew I was at home and that was exactly where I should stay. I did what he said and didn't move – twenty metres outside my front door.

A few weeks later the device was removed from my ankle and I was free to go anywhere, anytime. I drove to Yorkshire.

FIFTEEN

I thought that after my release from prison that I could get on with my life; get back to work without any more obstacles. I thought wrong.

What I had not bargained on was SOCA subjecting all of the co-defendants in the case to a proceeds of crime order. They were able to get me to unravel all my financial details, including how much I had in the bank and the value of my house, car and all my worldly goods, including quite sentimental and valuable family heirlooms. They also demanded copies of every invoice for the business and a description of the nature of every job I had done. A few weeks later they contacted my solicitor to insist that I pay them just under thirty thousand pounds. The order was designed to ensure that criminals didn't profit from the proceeds of their illegal activity. It was a ridiculous sum that they claimed was the amount I had made in profit while carrying out investigation and research tasks that they now classed as criminal. An absolute and total nonsense in reality. My life came to a grinding halt and I was under the total control of SOCA.

My solicitor sifted through their findings and ripped them to shreds. A number of the points related to totally legal and normal work and he was able to show that. He audited their claim sheets in forensic detail, questioning each and every entry and replying that only around a thousand pounds of what I had earned actually qualified as being the proceeds of illegal activity – and even that was questionable, as it was for work carried out against fraudsters on behalf of law firms and insurance companies. SOCA accepted the counter-offer and I sent them a cheque for a total of £970. It was a bit of a result really.

If only that had been the end of the matter, but SOCA weren't finished with me yet. They intended to impose an absurd number of restrictions on what I could do, under the terms of what was called a serious crime prevention order. It was draconian to say the least and I had to attend court for the order to be heard. The SOCA barrister was invited to make his case by the judge – who just so happened to be the same judge who had sentenced me to eight months in prison. It was not looking good from where I was standing. In a nutshell, the barrister said that the order would allow SOCA to monitor me and ensure that I was not committing crimes. It would prevent me from getting involved with more crimes in the future. That was one way of looking at it. The practical effect of the order was to restrict my life to an intolerable degree.

I would have to declare to SOCA that I owned and used just one mobile phone, one SIM card and one number only. I was to declare all the details and provide them with the email and password that I used for my online mobile phone bill. I was to be allowed to use a single computer equipped with pre-installed email software, I was to be allowed one email address and I was to provide SOCA with that email address and its password. I could have one landline, but all details of my phone account were to be declared to them, including the password I used to access the facility.

If I was to upgrade my phone or buy another computer I had to inform SOCA in writing immediately, stating the make and model of the equipment and even the colour (quite why the colour was required baffled me). Any new numbers, service providers or account details were also to be declared and if I joined a social networking provider such as Facebook or Twitter I had to provide SOCA with the details of my login name and password. If I was to get a telephone card then that had to be declared and all details provided. This was all to be sent to SOCA within five days of the order coming into force. Great Britain was turning into North Korea!

On top of these restrictions and notifications I was also told that I must have an email address that had either a .com or .co.uk suffix and I was not allowed to have access to any third-party email provider or right to use someone else's email. If I ever changed my name by deed poll then I was to inform SOCA immediately and update all my details as instructed.

I was told that I was to have no contact or communication with Danny – who had been our research bloke – in either a direct way or via a third party. I was also to tell SOCA twenty-four hours in advance if I was going to be leaving the property I was living in and this would include giving the addresses of any friends I might stay with or holiday locations.

Not enough? There was also a list of electronic devices that I was not allowed to have at all – such as a mobile VOIP (Voice Over Internet Protocol) device, two-way radio, any computer that would allow voice communication or a satellite phone.

All of these notifications were to be sent by recorded delivery and upon request by a SOCA officer I had to show the proof of postage receipt. If any of these restrictions were not complied with then I would put myself at risk of being sentenced to five years' imprisonment. It was basically a total lockdown of my life as I had known it. Oh – but I was to be allowed to keep a television set. This was actually specified on their order. Very generous.

Worst of all, I would not be permitted to be involved in any capacity in the business of private investigations, preventing me from working in an industry that I had been in since I had left the army. I did not know anything else and certainly did not have the right qualifications to apply for other jobs. This was looking bad. My barrister put these points across in his response and asked for the restrictions to be removed but to no avail: they remained on the list of requirements.

My barrister also highlighted that I had pleaded guilty to a charge that was at the lowest end of the scale of offending. He noted that I had been arrested on a much lesser charge but that SOCA had convinced the judge to raise a more serious offence. He pointed out that I had received a short, sharp shock by way of imprisonment and that my probation service report had stated quite categorically that I was unlikely to offend again. In effect, he argued, I had not been involved in serious crime. This sort of order should be reserved for those involved in drugs, firearms, people-trafficking, armed robbery, money-laundering, corruption and bribery. I had not been anywhere near this magnitude of serious crime.

He also pointed out that these kinds of orders were only to be imposed where there was a suggestion that someone would offend again and that they would be a risk to the public or become involved in serious crime. He contended that the order was only to come into force where there was a real or significant risk of such offences, otherwise the court could find itself in breach of Article eight of the Human Rights Act. This part of the Human Rights Act allows people to have a normal family life that is not interfered with by authorities or government agencies.

I recognised two SOCA officers who were sitting nearby with their barrister and the rest of their legal team. They were looking quite cocky and, obviously, they were looking forward to hearing the judge imposing the order on me. They were quite a vindictive lot and liked to think of themselves as the British version of the FBI – in fact, one of them had actually said that to Graham at one point. What a complete knob.

The SOCA barrister stood up and read out my name, my date of conviction and my offences and then delivered a generic statement to the effect that the court should have reasonable cause to believe that an order would protect the public by preventing, restricting or disrupting involvement by me – as the offender – in serious crimes in England and Wales.

The judge asked how much the SOCA barrister knew about the case and he replied that he had read the brief and the case notes. What came next was a complete but welcome shock.

The judge said that the barrister could not possibly be aware of the full complexities of the case as, if he had read the files in full, he would be aware that I had not committed any crimes and that I had merely employed and paid someone else to facilitate my requests. The judge told the barrister to leave the court for thirty minutes and acquaint himself with the content of the files and reminded everyone that it was he who had been the presiding judge in the original case – as if I could forget – and he knew the case intimately, as he had sentenced me. The barrister – soundly upbraided – stood up and went to leave the court to do his homework. But the judge had already reached his decision. 'Stop, don't bother,' he declared. He then looked over to me and my legal team and said, 'Mr Lewis, you may leave.' The order was thrown out.

My solicitor whispered, 'Result! Let's go and have a beer!'

I walked past the two SOCA officers, red-faced with rage and deeply unhappy about the judge's ruling. I looked at them, gave them a serious grin, smiled, and said, 'We're coming for the Manchester file now, boys,' and kept walking.

I was still on bail in relation to computer-hacking charges and my solicitor had also been informed by the Information Commissioner's Office (ICO) that they would be looking into other inquiries that SOCA had not brought to court which involved alleged breaches of the Data Protection Act. I thought, bloody hell – here we go again. In 2008, SOCA had looked into the activities of private investigators who were believed to be obtaining personal data. The matter had been referred to the ICO, who now intended to conduct further inquiries into the corporate clients who had commissioned the investigators' work.

One such client was a large insurance group who were suspected of instructing me to unlawfully obtain personal data that broke the Data Protection Act. In the original SOCA enquiry, they had decided not to include this information as the evidence was quite scant. The ICO requested that I submit to a voluntary interview under caution that was intended to determine my involvement in the offence. Any interview would be recorded and I would be entitled to have a copy – that was nice of them ... The ICO was not able to compel people to attend an interview and what to do would be my choice. The insurance group had dropped me like a hot potato after I was arrested, following years of them being my best client. I had carried out many sensitive jobs for them but was abruptly told not to make contact again. I owed them no favours, but I was never a snitch and I certainly was not going to give to the ICO information that they could use to prosecute me. My solicitor and I decided that we would not attend.

When my solicitor informed them of my decision not to attend as a 'witness' they then wrote to say that they would now be doing more work over the coming months to see if there was a case to prosecute me. This was just getting ridiculous.

Around this time, MPs were beginning to ask questions in parliamentary committees about our clients. If I had been investigated and jailed then surely the clients who employed or tasked me and my co-defendants were part of the larger conspiracy and should also be investigated. But the heads of SOCA refused to let the parliamentary home affairs committee see a list of our clients, to the concern of many.

Shortly after, SOCA itself suffered a bit of a shock. Their boss, Sir Ian Andrews resigned, having suddenly remembered that he had failed to declare that he and his wife were both directors of a company that provided consultancy advice to several businesses. It also emerged that Sir Ian's wife was a lawyer with a global private investigations company. They would have been competitors of ours. But in the world of the mighty and powerful you just tender your resignation, leave and no further action takes place. How incongruous. SOCA had a tendency to use several millions of pounds in an investigation that would recover one million and they were just not a financially viable organisation. They would also vanish, pretty much reborn in the form of the National Crime Agency (NCA), who now undertake similar roles.

I was contacted by my solicitor; I was to be questioned on bail at Charing Cross police station with regard to the long-standing charges of computer hacking. We could meet and have a chat before going into the session and go over any outstanding points. We always attended bail interviews as the questioning gave a good indication as to where the police were with their investigations – not to mention that I would have been in breach of my bail if I did not attend. That would have given them great pleasure as they could then re-arrest me and charge me yet again. I always attended and I always kept my hands in my pockets when the police officers greeted me; they would always try to shake hands and I would take the opportunity to stare at their outstretched hands and laugh. I always thought it helped to give me a little bit of control and ensured that the power balance was not always with them.

During this interview we learned that the police had not got very far and we got confirmation when, at length, the inspector turned off the recorder. He said he had permission from his boss to speak to me off the record – that was most unusual; in fact, it had never happened to me before. My solicitor agreed that it would be all right, but he would take notes and each side would write to the other to record what went on. It was agreed.

The inspector leaned back in his chair and put his hands behind his head, he was looking a bit forlorn, stared at me and sighed. 'I have sixteen officers working on this case and a bill mounting up towards the millions,' he admitted. 'And all I have to show for it, so far, is Rob Lewis.'

He wanted to know if there was any way I could help them out by providing names of my collaborators. In a nutshell – after all this time, they had nothing they could charge me with (otherwise they would have), and they had nobody else that they could bring into the investigation. Now they had to justify the manpower and the budget. I asked if I could have a word with my solicitor alone, they agreed and they left the room.

My solicitor knew that there was nobody else involved in the case. It was just me, as I had been working alone. He planned to ask what they were willing to offer in exchange for my co-operation. It was going to be a game of poker and right now we obviously held the better cards. When the inspector returned, my solicitor insisted that any offer they would make would have to be written. We would consider it and get back to them.

They were not that keen on this approach and did not commit to the idea: they just wanted me to tell them how our kind of operations were run and who else was involved. But we were clear. That was not going to happen without some sort of incentive. The inspector said that he would have to go back to his boss to discuss this matter and would get back to me and my solicitor in the next few days.

I soon heard that the computer-hacking charges were being dropped; there was insufficient evidence to secure a conviction and the CPS had decided not to pursue the case. I had been on bail for five years, a ridiculous amount of time. I now just had the ICO to deal with and I would be finished – free, at last. That news was not long coming and when my solicitor got in touch it was again with good news. The file of evidence submitted to the ICO prosecutor and external counsel had now been reviewed. They sent this comment to my solicitor: 'There is cogent evidence which satisfies the evidential test in relation to your client. However, in our view, it would be oppressive to seek to prosecute him for matters of this age, when he has already been prosecuted for closely related conduct in the same period and served a prison sentence as a result. It follows that in our view the public interest test is not satisfied in relation to your client.' They even thanked me for my patience.

I went into town and bought a bottle of Moët & Chandon champagne and raised several glasses that evening. I now had no charges hanging over my head. Life was good, at last.

EPILOGUE

'*It is not the critic who counts; not the man who points out how the strong man stumbles, or where the doer of deeds could have done them better. The credit belongs to the man who is actually in the arena, whose face is marred by dust and sweat and blood; who strives valiantly; who errs, who comes short again and again, because there is no effort without error and shortcoming; but who does actually strive to do the deeds; who knows great enthusiasms, the great devotions; who spends himself in a worthy cause; who at the best knows in the end the triumph of high achievement, and who at the worst, if he fails, at least fails while daring greatly, so that his place shall never be with those cold and timid souls who neither know victory nor defeat.*'

Theodore Roosevelt